London Fragments

London Fragments

A Literary Expedition

by
Rüdiger Görner

Translated by
Debra Marmor and Herbert Danner

HAUS PUBLISHING
London
 ArmchairTraveller

Copyright © 2007 Rüdiger Görner

Translation copyright © 2007 Debra Marmor and Herbert Danner

First published in Great Britain in 2007 by
Haus Publishing Limited
70 Cadogan Place
London SW1X 9AH
www.hauspublishing.co.uk

This paperback edition published in 2010 by
The Armchair Traveller
at the bookHaus

Originally published as *Londoner Fragmente: Literarische Streifzüge*
© 2003 Patmos Verlag GmbH & Co. KG Artemis & Winkler Verlag, Düsseldorf

The moral rights of the author have been asserted.

A CIP catalogue record for this book is available from the British Library

ISBN 978-1-906598-73-0

Typeset in Garamond by MacGuru Ltd
info@macguru.org.uk
Printed and bound in the UK by CPI Mackays, Chatham ME5 8TD

Contents

For Jocelyn

Acknowledgements

I should like to thank a number of people without whom *London Fragments* would not exist or who have provided additional pieces of information or useful corrections: Kim Landgraf (formerly of Artemis & Winkler, Düsseldorf), who commissioned and supported the book in the first place; the team of my London publisher as well as my translators Debra Marmor and Herbert Danner for their sheer competence and enthusiasm; and Peter Sager and Ulrich Broich for valuable comments. But, most importantly, I wish to express my deepest gratitude to my wife, Jocelyn Görner, for unfailing support in all matters of life – in London and elsewhere.

The path that leads the wanderer to the city does not bear its name.

Nikolaus von Kues, 1462

I have seen the strangest thing the world can show a curious soul, I have seen it and am still amazed – this stone wall of houses and between them the pressing stream of living human faces with all their colourful passions, with their horrifying haste in love, hunger and hate, is frozen in my memory – I am speaking of London.

Heinrich Heine, *Englische Fragmente*, 1828

He memorises entire cities before he sees them. He loves the names of streets that he has not yet walked. He is dreaming of them. Their names are always more alive than the places themselves.

Elias Canetti, 1992

I have read enough descriptions, both fiction and non-fiction, to know that London does not fit on the page. London sprawls, mutates, deceives; wears one garb by day and another by night; smiles when the sun shines and grimaces in the rain.

Monica Ali, 2006

Preface to the English Edition

I suppose it is presumptuous for me, a foreign author, to call my *London Fragments* an homage to this most fascinating, puzzling and bewildering metropolis. Perhaps less presumptuous is the implicit intention of this book, written as it is by a German, to draw attention to at least some of the great German-speaking Anglophiles of the past who regarded London as the obvious focal point of their pro-English sentiments. To get the measure of a German Anglophile you have to imagine my first English teacher at a grammar school in the depths of the Black Forest. She was a vicar's wife from the minor aristocracy, who would drink her cup of tea at five o'clock sharp, enlighten us on the difference between 'dinner' and 'supper' and make us sing 'God save the Queen' on St George's Day. 'Things English' were not to be criticised in her classes. England, with London as the pinnacle of the English-speaking world, was presented to us innocent children of the deep and dark southwest of Germany as the model of all civilization and the cradle of democracy. Since I came to London in 1981 I have indeed never ceased to be fascinated by this incommensurable metropolis, even though I soon became disillusioned with Thatcherism which left too many lasting scars on the mentality of both the city and the country.

Even though this book is not about politics in London I should like to say that one of the most remarkable and heartening developments in the capital is the re-establishment of London's administrative and political autonomy which had been tragically, and by continental European standards unlawfully, taken away in the 1980s.

Perhaps there should be a minimum length for a book on London; 800 pages seems about right. Or if one considers the time it should take to write it, I would imagine somewhere between 25 years and a lifetime. By these standards *London Fragments* would have to fail. However, this book is a testament to my passion for and irritation with this mega-city. By chance, the English edition was completed exactly a quarter of a century after I first came to these shores, which means that these reflections on London had spent a long time maturing before they were written up in 2003/2004. It also means that I believe that a look at London from the perspective of literature might better tame this urban beast and beauty.

My *London Fragments* therefore documents the illusion that this city can be tamed by words; that adequate expressions for its incommensurability can be found; and that London cares about the way in which it is represented in literature. Of course, by any standards this is a total fiction. The notion that cities can be read like novels should not hide the fact that we also need to listen to them, even though they do not listen to us. Cities are centres of indifference and anonymity. They are buzzing hubs of activity and cultural diversity but also focal points of suffering, deprivation and despair. In essence, they are unmanageable. And yet they radiate a sense of structure and the self-explanatory rhythms of life.

When I say 'they' I mean, of course, London, this city of cities, admittedly still less chic than Paris, less charged with mythology than Rome or Athens, but more diverse than Tokyo and less frenzied than New York. London is a synthesis of everything and everybody but what to call its common denominator is an open question; least of all would it be Englishness. It seems familiar and strange at one and the same time, cosy in some parts and alienating in others.

In short, it is the stuff that literature is made of, fiction and poetry that fluctuates between reality and imagination guided by strangely fascinating people who are represented in the following pages by the 'Lady in Yellow'. In fact, there was a harbinger of this figure in previous literature about London: when Heinrich Heine, that towering figure of 19th-century European poetry, came to London in 1827 he pretended to have encountered an ominous 'Yellow Man' on the barge that brought him up the Thames to London. He hoped to make him his guide to London but soon after disembarking he lost sight of him. Not so in my case: the 'Lady in Yellow' keeps pointing me in various, often opposite, directions in this city. I assume that in her quiet back garden in some noisy London district there must be a little menagerie with a small unicorn in its midst.

Truth be told, *London Fragments* was also written as an homage to Heinrich Heine and his *Englische Fragmente,* not because of his relentless mocking of the English character (Heine never forgave the English for their attitude towards food and for having defeated his life-long idol, Napoleon) but because of his stylistic and compositional finesse, the subtlety of his observations and the sheer brilliance of his associative reflections.

When I started writing *London Fragments*, nature came to visit the capital in the form of countryside protesters, and the year in which the English version of this book was completed began with a dramatically different invasion of nature into the urban setting. A northern bottlenose whale, hopelessly lost, swam up the Thames, creating a feeling of sheer helplessness and impotent compassion everywhere. A similar spectacle was recorded by John Evelyn in 1658: 'A large whale was taken betwixt my land abutting on the Thames and Greenwich, which drew an infinite concourse to see it, by water, horse, coach and on foot, from London and all parts.' Compassion for sea creatures was less developed in those days. 'It would have destroyed all the boats, but [...] after a long conflict, it was killed with a harping iron, struck in the head, out of which spouted blood and water.' Our 11-year-old 18-foot female whale, a Moby Dick in search of a new Herman Melville, died of convulsions.

There are many other literary guides through London, as well as the most recent London-based fiction, in particular Ian McEwan's fascinating novel *Saturday* (2005) with the extraordinary demonstration against the threatened invasion of Iraq as the backdrop of this masterpiece. One should also allow oneself to be lead through London by Maureen Duffy's novel *Capital* (1975), experience London's aura from the historical perspective Lawrence Norfolk evoked so masterly in *Lempriere's Dictionary* (1991), add to one's always frustrating, if not humiliating, experience of the London Underground Barbara Vine's fictional contribution to this precarious and suffocating underworld, so unworthy of this great metropolis, *King Solomon's Carpet* (1992), and accompany at least one of Geoff Nicholson's London-mad characters on his explorations of this urban phenomenon in *Bleeding London* (1997).

However, an entire chapter should be devoted to Monica Ali's incomparable examination of London's ethnic East End, her novel *Brick Lane* (2003), one of the most fascinating depictions to date of the capital's multicultural diversity in general and of the Bengali community in particular, not to mention its radical potential. It is only since my appointment to Queen Mary College, this powerhouse of intellectual innovation, in 2004 that I begin to discover for myself the exceptional richness of the opportunities and challenges of London's East End. Previously it was mainly Harold Pinter's reminiscence of the Jewish East End of his youth, *The Dwarfs* (1960) and, more recently, Gilda O'Neill's memoirs of life in Cockney London, *My East End* (1999), that helped shape my conception of this area.

Having said this, it was gratifying to find Monica Ali sharing my enthusiasm for Virginia Woolf's essays on London (*The London Scene*, 1975), which I allude to in Chapter 6 of this book. While *London Fragments* was being translated I found Ali's delightful essay 'After Woolf' in *The Guardian Weekend* (May 2006) in which she describes how she was 'idling in Woolf's footsteps'. As she explained, 'trying to get the measure of London is futile. Better to do as Woolf does in her 1930s essays on London, written for *Good Housekeeping* magazine, and catch at thoughts and feelings, the immediate perception of things, so as to be able to say, like Lily Briscoe in *To the Lighthouse*, "Yes, I have had my vision"'.

Such a 'vision' can require some major sacrifices. So, for example, references to most of this City's treasure houses, galleries and museums are missing in my *London Fragments*. Nor will the reader find cinemas, concert halls, hospital wards, or the large cemeteries and small churchyards (for most continental Europeans coming to this country the most desolate and God-forsaken places imaginable) – all these fertile grounds of literature.

Ever so much is still to be discovered in this city; so much is unaccountably lost. We are what we see, hear, remember and imagine. We are inhabited by images and sounds, 'soundscapes' of London as opposed to *Greensleeves*, that irresistible melody of another world that is, however, still contained in ours. Oh, London, this perpetual wake-up call to (literary) life.

Rüdiger Görner

January 2007

1

Arriving in the Nowhere by the Thames

Approaching London at night: as if floating in on shadows, perforated by millions of lights. The holding pattern in a droning albatross over Albion's urban centrepiece. Albion, England's Celtic name, meaning 'White Land' – white like the legendary chalk cliffs of Dover.

As an unknown captain and his autopilot circle us over London hundreds, thousands of people are arriving: at Paddington, Waterloo and Victoria stations, at the innumerable bus stops and Tube stations, in the maelstrom of road traffic, and even in rare cases at piers along the Thames. Arrival is an illusion, the illusion of ever being able to arrive, because London is the metropolis of the gyratory system. And 'gyratory system' means: avoidance of a clear sense of direction, a prerequisite for any arrival.

London is also the city of fly-by-night luggage merchants. What other city has so many improvised kiosks with suitcases, most often next to newsagents or in front of Underground stations? As if the vendors hope that the spectacular headlines about the all-time low of the world situation would induce passers-by to quickly acquire a new piece of luggage in order to be able to escape somewhere else.

And so we continue to circle above London. During a night flight it seems endless. A casual exchange of words develops in passing with the passenger in the next seat; mostly meaningless banter, as no one whom you might have spotted while queuing to check in and hoped might be assigned that seat ever sits there. After all, such an ideal travel acquaintance would be as good as a sizeable lottery win; the equivalent of arriving before the arrival time, like breaking through the holding pattern. Oh, you also read Nick Hornby? Oh, you are still reading Heine? Or: how long we might still have to circle? One talks of turbulence survived during a descent from 10,000 metres or of the newest statistics that claim London on average grows by 40,000 inhabitants each year, or about the weather forecast for your stay north or south of the Thames.

The actual ideal travel acquaintance, at least while circling in the holding pattern, clad in astonishingly contrasting tones of yellow (amazing how a single colour can vary!), smiles, knows quite a bit about the city without revealing too much. I pretend as though I were on my first visit to London; concealing the fact that I have lived here for over 20 years. The lady in Seat B hints, as the aircraft prepares to land, a certain interest in meeting up again, recommends this museum and that restaurant, then makes her farewells as she leaves Row 16 without having made any commitment.

Landed. Heathrow, Stansted, London City Airport – or had we turned toward Gatwick? One and the same. They are interchangeable. London, here is London. Somehow it seems inappropriate to simply refer to London as a 'city'. London is an amalgam, a macrocosm, chaos dressed up as if it were manageable. London represents flickering urbanity and yet always manages to provide a surprising sense of intimacy, square by square. These squares were originally trademarks of the city. Maps of London from the 17th century show a world of clearly demarcated little gardens. 'House and garden', often demonstratively too small, intended for life at closest proximity, but one's own space. It would appear they tried to create manageable housing conditions.

Arriving in London is not merely ticking the box. As mentioned, I have been trying to live here for over two decades and each time I arrive it is as though it is the first time – after every journey, every day. Arriving in London is a project.

The city break, that most bizarre absurdity of contemporary tourism, continues to enjoy great popularity: Prague in three days, Budapest in two (one day for Buda, one for Pest), St Petersburg in two and a half days (half a day to queue for the Hermitage), Amsterdam, Madrid and anywhere else that can be done in 36 hours. But London is different. Whoever approaches London is threatened by a life sentence. This city does not seduce immediately, but rather over the long term. Its ability to penetrate is like a slow-release drug.

Paris is the city for love at first sight. Rome is known as the capital of sensual living. Venice is art that has become a city. And Bruges is a huge museum of commerce elevated to art in the early modern era. In contrast, London's effect is one of 'inexhaustible presence', as Harry Graf Kessler, one of the great minds of Europe of the early 20th century, a true Anglophile and 'cultural networker' *avant la lettre*, noted in his diary in July 1921.

Admittedly you also travel to London to view the historic buildings. And at first glance one might say: There can't be so much history. The dense agglomeration of places of interest seems overwhelming (even if there are more in Vienna's Erstem Bezirk), while at Buckingham Palace, that graceless example of boxy Victorian architecture, you might actually see the living version of that wax figure you had admired a few hours earlier at Madame Tussaud's.

But that is not it. London's ability to get under your skin has relatively little in common with Tower Bridge and Big Ben. This chaotic system called London, this functioning urbanism always on the verge of collapse, lures us with the offer of anonymity, interspersed with apparent intimacy. Something else magically attracts – the name 'London', of course. For a German speaker it suggests a constant state of arrival when pronounced in English 'lundon', which in German sounds like the equivalent of 'to land'. Compare that to 'Londres' or 'Londra'? Perhaps it is the German version, with the two ringing, fulsome, equally emphasised vowels, which give the appropriate weight to this urban hydra.

Every London visitor claims to find himself enchanted, left breathless and exhausted with amazement. That is how it should be. After all, you want to be able to tell yourself that you can sense some sort of redeeming value in this capital of overcharging. Exactly what is it that astounds?

Perhaps it is the time lag, or not immediately feeling upset in the face of the unspeakable social contrasts. These are apparent despite the fact that, since the days of the 'Iron Lady', sporadic efforts, sometimes approaching human rights violations, have been made to remove beggars from the principal tourist areas of London. Social reform of a different sort.

A visitor finds himself continually disturbed, bewildered even by the unbelievable number of security cameras on nearly every street corner. From Camden Town to Notting Hill Gate, from Brixton to Neasden: security cameras. Imagine for a moment the endless images of London these cameras record, the abundance of pictures that are produced every minute. The camera as city security service. Imagine yourself sitting in front of monitors in some control room somewhere and following these pictures of life in a street or at a traffic roundabout. I will always remember the sight of one security camera, high on a mast, where one of the oversized London crows had lighted and in typical crow fashion tiredly stretched out its wings – one of them directly across the camera's lens. London as the capital of security fanatics. The discretely obvious manner in which alarm systems are mounted on houses in most neighbourhoods provides a clue to the economic standard of their residents.

I am aware of only two well known German-speaking visitors who made virtually no mention of their visit to London: Johann Caspar Schiller in 1748, father of the classic writer, and Thomas Mann, who indignantly remarked on the poor food at the Savoy on the Strand during his visit in 1947. The poet Rainer Maria Rilke did not even come. The thought of London repulsed him. When he was still Auguste Rodin's private secretary there was talk for a while of organising a Rodin exhibition in London. Preparations for the visit were looming for Rilke, but the plans came to naught as the passionate yet ever-critical poet, a Parisian by choice, noted with satisfaction. For him and his relationship with urban spheres, despite the fascination that city auras held for him, the importance was the confession in his *Stunden-Buch* (*Book of Hours*): he despised big cities; the great ones no longer truly existed; they were all frauds, telling untruths in their silence and their noise.

By the way, one should *never* ride in an open-topped double-decker tourist bus. Their carefully arranged routes virtually guarantee not seeing the 'real London'. Rather, entrust yourself to any regular bus, preferably a double-decker, and let yourself drift, looking from the upper-deck seats through the mostly curtainless windows into flats with their often sparse furnishings and their bare light bulbs dangling in the middle of the room. Bicycle and ironing board in the living room. Poverty precisely because the people in these flats live for nothing else but to pay their mortgage or rent, which even for the most run-down accommodation can border on stratospheric. Southeast England alone has a higher per capita debt level than any other country in Europe. On the other hand, there are also only a few neighbourhoods in European cities like London's Hampstead, where according to the latest survey the *average* annual per capita income (from infant to old man) is around £100,000. What fertile soil for literature!

'When a man is tired of London, he is tired of life ...' One of the many well-known aphorisms of Samuel Johnson, who was always coming up with pithy sayings. To this day, he continues to be regarded as *the* literary authority on 18th-century London, despite the fact that he was a son of the Midlands (he was from Lichfield). In 1738 he published an epic poem entitled *London* in which he lamented the corruption of the city's soul and denounced its poverty: 'This mournful Truth is ev'ry where confest/ slow rises worth,/ by poverty deprest ... '

That is how it has always been. People moved 'from outside' into London, only to then yearn for the rural idyll which they attempted to simulate by creating the green patches of the squares and their tiny gardens. The renaissance of the English pastoral, that essence of all that is English, was repeatedly evoked in the middle of London, from Samuel Johnson to Roger Scruton and Peter Ackroyd. Something always to be remembered: London, regardless whether pronounced with a Yorkshire or Devonshire accent, is often a curse from the perspective of the provincial English, or indeed anyone from the rest of the British Isles. London stands for the arrogance of a capital city that has patronised the countryside for centuries.

Oddly enough, while I am writing about London here in the autumn of 2002, a rural protest movement, in some respects resembling that of the late Middle Ages, is beginning to gather against London. It calls itself the Countryside Alliance, actually a true alliance of country dwellers, a home guard against the City. More than a quarter of a million of them marched on London on the penultimate Sunday in September 2002 to demonstrate for the preservation of the country way of life. Ostensibly demonstrating to preserve foxhunting, they were bringing attention to the pauperisation of the agrarian economy and the forestry industry, the destruction of the rural social infrastructure with its pubs and small shops, and the indifference of this city of millions to the source of its food. They were also making clear their objection to the 'suburbanisation' of the areas surrounding London (the commuter belt has now grown to a radius of between 50 and 100 miles) and exorbitant property prices, driven up by commuters moving into rural communities. But this is no farmers' revolt with pitchforks and muck rakes against the Horse Guards. Farmers and landed gentry, as well as former townsfolk who moved to the country, are uniting against the cynicism of the City. They are demanding that the urban population become aware of their concerns, even going so far as stopping traffic for an entire Sunday.

I have in front of me a local paper from the borough of Camden, which reports on road closures on the day of the great demonstration. The paper is printed in the following languages: English, Farsi, Urdu, Bengali, Somali, Yoruba, Chinese (Mandarin), Albanian, French, Portuguese, Spanish, Turkish and Arabic. Camden, in particular, has experience in matters of country-city issues. 'The country' began here in Dickens' time, and a small farm holding remains as a reminder. The London Zoo, in Regent's Park near Camden, the most neglected city zoo one can imagine, keeps a single lonely dairy cow along with a costly milking system. Camden has also erected a memorial to Richard Cobden, that great Victorian agricultural reformer and chief opponent of the Corn Laws, who introduced important social reforms during Queen Victoria's reign. A recent survey in Camden Town showed that only 0.02 per cent of respondents had any idea to whom this bronze monument at the southern end of Camden Town was dedicated.

Countryside versus City. English literature thrived on this contrast for centuries. Imagine a conversation between Charles Dickens, the most urban of English writers, and Thomas Hardy, the good man from Dorset and advocate of the countryside. The young Hardy, who practised as an architect in London, once met Dickens in a coffee house in Charing Cross, but no conversation ensued between them, he later recalled, long after he had started to digest the hell of the supposed rural idyll in his novels.

Countryside and the myth of primitive nature against the nonchalantly smug or artificially excited city: I am reminded of Ted Hughes and finally comprehend, after his far too premature death in 1998, how much this everlasting discussion adds to the meaning of his poetry. His poem *Epiphany*, in *The Birthday Letters*, is set at the entrance to Chalk Farm Underground Station, near Camden Town and tells of an unexpected encounter with a 'young fellow', who holds a fox cub 'buttoned into the top of his jacket' and is trying to sell it. An armload of comical wilderness in the chaos of the city. Offered for sale for £1 sterling. But the 'I' in the poem continues:

> *I let that fox-cub go. I tossed it back*
> *Into the future*
> *Of a fox-cub in London and I hurried*
> *Straight on and dived as if escaping*
> *Into the Underground.*

Whoever wants to see something in London, to see London, or who wants to understand aspects of this juggernaut, needs an inner compass as a tour guide to insanity. Take Ted Hughes' urban fox as an example. London is no city of destinations; rather it is one of diversions and wrong turns. Whoever decides to go, for example, in search of Samuel Johnson's house near Fleet Street and then even manages to arrive there promptly, has understood nothing of London's unwritten rules. Under these conditions, we set off on our way, keeping in mind the reading material of my Lady in Yellow.

2

(Un-) Real City –
London as a Literary Theme

If you approach a large city by way of literature, then you can hardly avoid encountering a mythical version of it. It is basically the myth of Atlantis, the legendary sunken city, which we repeatedly discover anew. Or do we reinvent Babylon, or attempt to rescue what is left of heavenly Jerusalem every time we write about a city? Wherever our mythological preferences may lie, we continually seem to seek a narrative style that allows us to communicate what is essentially indescribable – the metropolis.

In the digital age this search for the mythological origins of the city finds its equivalent in the virtual existence of the global village. Through the Internet we can all feel like citizens of the world, whilst savouring our electronically enforced isolation in front of our various screens.

Be that as it may, we associate various styles of narrative about metropolitan existence with various cities. Narrative recreation of city structures is one of the most important challenges in literary history. One only has to think of Dostoevsky's St Petersburg, Joyce's Dublin, Döblin's Berlin, Grass' Danzig and of course Dickens' London. But the most individual, possibly even most imaginative, approximation in the body of city literature came from Italo Calvino in his novel, *Le città invisibili* (1972), in which he lets the Venetian explorer Marco Polo report on the adventures he had in cities on his journey to the emperor of the Tartars, Kublai Khan. Calvino's narrator categorises the different cities as 'subtle', 'everlasting' and 'hidden', in which he intersperses his daydreams with urban realities. The imagination of the narrator thus creates a space for the reader, which he can begin to inhabit. But these city tales by Calvino's Marco Polo have another meaning. The more he talks and the more the Tartar emperor begins to participate in these tales, the more unreal the Khan's actual political power begins to appear.

In some ways this applies to all city tales. The more we read or hear about a city, the more improbable and perhaps even unimportant its reality begins to appear. Take for example The Old Curiosity Shop in London's Portsmouth Street not far from the Strand. Dickens' fictionalisation of this place lent it an alternate reality, which differs considerably from the actual, rather disappointing-looking shop. The fictional reality satisfies our desire for an imaginative embodiment of that which is portrayed. This recounted reality endows this entirety, the place as well as those 'curious' things which are found there, with something enduring.

In many respects the most comprehensive and precise London tale is found in music. I refer to a composition by the young Ralph Vaughan Williams called *A London Symphony*, which he completed in 1914. With this one of his two symphonies, English music found its connection to the modern age. Each of the four movements introduces a contrasting theme, which illustrates the hustle and bustle of the city, but also includes moments of almost eerie silence. The first and last measures of the symphony evoke a damp foggy London, as we know it from Turner's and Whistler's famous paintings, which often portray the Thames. But the London of the young Vaughan Williams is a place of sharp contrasts and rapidly changing moods. Decidedly melodious phrases, which seem to express a certain equanimity, alternate with suspenseful sequences full of nervous petulance, which are then replaced by humorous passages that are reminiscent of the world of the East End Cockney. We hear the background noise of the pubs and the chimes of Big Ben and finally deathly silence. Vaughan Williams had initially intended to name his composition the 'Symphony of a Londoner', suggesting that this music represented abstractions of the sound world of London. However that may be, this symphony has a narrative quality which is certainly comparable to conventional London narratives.

Let us not forget that a young student from Boston by the name of T S Eliot also saw London for the first time in 1914, when he was returning from studying in Marburg. What was intended to be a visit became a passion for London that was to determine the rest of his life. Barely eight years after his arrival in London, he wrote *The Waste Land*, a work that was to revolutionise our understanding of modern poetry and also began to write the myth of London anew:

> *Unreal City,*
> *Under the brown fog of a winter dawn,*
> *A crowd flowed over London Bridge, so many,*
> *I had not thought death had undone so many.*
> *Sighs, short and infrequent, were exhaled,*
> *And each man fixed his eyes before his feet.*
> *Flowed up the hill and down King William Street,*
> *To where Saint Mary Woolnoth kept the hours*
> *With a dead sound on the final stroke of nine.*

Shortly after his arrival in London in September 1914 Eliot divulged in a letter: 'I find it quite possible to work in this atmosphere. The noises of such a city so large as London don't distract one much; they become attached to the city and depersonalise themselves.' London appeared to him at first glance 'to be foreign, but hospitable, or rather tolerant, and perhaps does not so demand to be understood as does Paris'.

This is a remarkable claim, as it introduces a thought in Eliot's writings that was to become one of his most important: modern writing is grounded in the process of depersonalisation. And a city like London, whose tolerance or perhaps indifference makes few demands on its visitors, seemed to him the ideal place to achieve exactly this in his writing.

Comparisons between Paris, London and Berlin, this frequently researched triangle of rivalries and vanities, are essentially pointless considering the conspicuously distinctive characteristics of these cities. Paris is certainly omnipresent in British prose ever since Laurence Sterne's famous Paris episodes in his *Sentimental Journey*. Berlin, however, figures far less frequently in British prose, with the exception of Christopher Isherwood's novel *Goodbye to Berlin*, Ian Walker's adventures in East and West Berlin, *Zoo Station*, and Philip Hensher's novel *Pleasured*, a description of Berlin in 1988 as a city of escapists and the (self-) obsessed. French authors, on the other hand, do not seem to count London or Berlin amongst their preferred places. The German contribution to the literature of Paris is primarily restricted to Rilke's experimental novel, *Die Aufzeichnungen des Malte Laurids Brigge*, and more recently, Undine Gruenter's impressive Paris fantasies. German-speaking authors also seem to be rather hard-pressed in regard to London. The major exceptions are the poet Heinrich Heine and the novelist Theodor Fontane, who attempted to convey their London experiences in the form of fragmentary or mosaic-like notes. This they did literally in the footsteps of Karl Phillip Moritz whose *Reisen eines Deutschen in England im Jahr 1782* (trans. London 1795: *Travels, chiefly on foot, through several parts of England*) was the early measure for all future literary tourism in London and England by Germans.

When the great German dramatist Friedrich Hebbel tried a narrative report on London with a broader view in June 1862 – the intent was an overview for the *Leipziger Illustrierte Zeitung* – he quickly admitted defeat. The social drama, which he reported precisely in his letters, surpassed even his imagination. He called London a Hobbesian 'Leviathan' that both presided over and perpetuated unspeakable discrepancies between fairytale riches and shocking poverty.

But what about London as *the* defining theme amongst the British literati? London enters the stage of modern literature through the *Diaries* of Samuel Pepys and his description of the Great Fire in the City in 1666, as well as with Daniel Defoe's *Journal of the Plague Year 1665*. In other words, the real and fictitious diarists at the time attempted to deal with the phenomenon of the city in catastrophic times. Just 200 years earlier, the poet William Dunbar could still refer to London as 'Flower of all Cities'; now, however, at the beginning of the modern age, it seemed to be suffocating in dirt, even if this later turned out to be fertile soil.

Writing about London meant to proceed 'intra urbem' in those days, directly into city life and thus the serious social issues. The more elevated discourse on the city, the 'supra urbem', remained the preserve of the literature of Rome, as the introduction to Thomas Mann's novel *Der Erwählte* ('The Holy Sinner', 1951), shows. Authors perceived London as a decidedly worldly and profane city from the very beginning. Consequently, that is where Defoe's immodest protagonist Moll Flanders pursues her carnal business. And 200 years later, Virginia Woolf would admit that she saw the streets of London through different eyes after she had reread Defoe's novel.

Defoe had established the perception of London as a body politic. The first half of the 18th century differentiated amongst three forms of London descriptions: those in prose, those in pictures and those on the stage. It was the street that gave wings to the artist's imagination. As a result, the poet John Gay published a London guide entitled *Trivia, or the Art of Walking the Streets of London*, which in many respects prepared him for his masterpiece – the libretto for *The Beggar's Opera*.

Through this revolt against fashionable Italian opera, as represented by Handel, Gay elevated the song of the alley to the level of an operatic travesty. Gay's *Beggar's Opera* represented a triumph of sensual vulgarity over courtly art. Or to put it another way, London's 'body' clamoured against foreign cultural influences, perhaps for the last time. But during the following decades this aspect of cultural life in London changed dramatically: cosmopolitan urbanity became its defining characteristic and thus also the reciprocal integration of cultural streams in the metropolis.

William Hogarth's drawings and engravings created the pictorial analogue to Gay's literary depiction of London's streets. His tableaux of London life, stretching from the illustrations for the *Beggar's Opera* to *The Enraged Musician, Gin Lane, Industry and Idleness, Southwark Fair* and of course *A Rake's Progress*, taken together represent a story in images. They have substantially shaped our perception of 18th-century London. Hogarth's achievement was repeatedly appreciated, particularly by foreign visitors, such as the scientist, champion of the Enlightenment and wit Georg Christoph Lichtenberg of Göttingen, whose descriptions of Hogarth's engravings provided a substitute for the never-written 18th-century German novel of London.

The artist and writer in 18th-century London discovered that his city was 'legible'. Through its streets, social distinctions and personalities the city offered a unique 'text' that one only needed to pick up and transfer to the medium of art. To the degree that one takes the metaphor of the body for this metropolis literally, one could argue that more and more London-obsessed authors contributed to the great autobiographical project, so to speak, named 'London'. In this sense, one could also suggest that London more or less hired its ghostwriters for its autobiographical project in the form of Defoe or Dickens. Since Peter Ackroyd published his extensive study, *London*, with the descriptive subtitle, '*The Biography*', in 2000, this thought seems markedly less absurd.

During the 19th century London moved to centre stage in English literature after Thomas de Quincey confessed that only opium provided him with temporary release from this maddening city with Oxford Street as its, and his, 'strong-hearted stepmother'. The Victorian novel, represented by Dickens, Thackeray, George Eliot, Meredith and Trollope, not to mention Wilkie Collins and George Gissing, responded to the increasing complexities of the social structure of the metropolis, which by then had become the focal point of the Empire. London had now also become the object of quasi-scientific research, such as Charles Knight's multi-volume study, which appeared in the 1870s and 1880s. Other authors, for instance Charles Manby Smith, insisted on representing the more likeable side of London. In 1857 Smith published his book, *The Little World of London*, while on the other side of the Channel the scandalous *Fleurs du Mal* by Charles Baudelaire and Gustave Flaubert's no less daring *Madame Bovary* appeared. But the title does not quite meet the intention of the book because Smith was now speaking of a London that suffered from noise and was in danger of losing its pleasant aspects.

In his 'biography' of London, Ackroyd certainly points out that the city and its inhabitants defended their right to noise. Noise and intrusive sounds of all sorts were, if you will, the acoustic emblems of this metropolis, which found expression, for example, in Richard Henry Horne's *Memoirs of a London Doll*, which appeared in 1846. This volume can claim a very special place in London literature. Its reader experiences the riches of London through the eyes of a doll that was made by an impoverished tradesman with the last of what he had. Horne himself was a journalist and writer, who worked in Fleet Street for the newspapers *Daily News* and *Household Words* under Dickens' direction. Later he was appointed to a government commission, which was to investigate the issue of child labour. His report about this sorry state of affairs, incidentally, led to one of the first humane labour laws in England. London from the doll's perspective seemed a dubious place. The same applied to the view of this monstrosity on the Thames by split personalities like a Jekyll and Hyde (1886); for in the eyes of Robert Louis Stevenson, the author of this legendary novel, London had long since become the breeding ground for schizophrenic figures.

But it is worth remembering that one could still write of London as an idyllic place at the beginning of the 19th century without appearing to be fanciful. That is how *the* Romantic poet of England, William Wordsworth, depicted an urban pastoral that practically mythologizes London in his September 1802 poem,

> Composed upon Westminster Bridge:
> *Earth has not anything to show more fair:*
> *Dull would he be of soul who could pass by*
> *A sight so touching in its majesty:*
> *This city now doth, like a garment, wear*
> *The beauty of the morning; silent, bare,*
> *Ships, towers, domes, theatres, and temples lie*

Open unto the fields, and to the sky;
All bright and glittering in the smokeless air.
Never did the sun more beautifully steep
In his splendour, valley, rock or hill;
Ne'er saw I, never felt, a calm so deep!
The river glideth at his own sweet will:
Dear God! the very houses seem asleep;
And all that mighty heart is lying still!

This is the idyll as opposed to the capital of noise. Wordsworth's London portrait resembles a poetic still life, approaching the myth of an idealised connection between nature and urban civilisation, unlike the poem *London* by Samuel Johnson mentioned at the outset, which criticises the city. When Wordsworth's poem celebrated its 200th birthday recently, the London tabloid, *The Evening Standard,* published a detailed evaluation. The reviewer wrote a critique of what he saw as a mediocre romantic concoction by a third-class lyricist.

Over the course of the 19th century London tales had attained a quasi-mythical status. London had established itself as a continuing literary project, which, in principle, did not need to be questioned anymore. In Anthony Trollope's novel, *The Way We Live Now* (1874/5), London even becomes the 'full authority' quoted in all questions of living. It is a novel about social climbers who become bankrupt, and of those who have come down in the world, who sell their values: human comedy and the belief in vanities on the banks of the Thames.

The *flâneur* is more of an exception in London literature because London has squares but no boulevards, clubs but no street cafés. The London dandy sparkles indoors; he does not take a step outside because, as Oscar Wilde felt, exercise ruins the wit. Perhaps Charles Dickens best personified the London *flâneur*, although that would not be quite accurate. A *flâneur* is typified by a leisurely, pleasurable gait, a pace unfamiliar to Dickens who was always in a hurry. At the beginning of his collection of essays, *Sketches by Boz* (1836), the street became the definitive narrative perspective and the *flâneur*, or better still the walker, was declared the only legitimate narrator.

The London *flâneur* was the theme in another essay at this time, Edgar Allan Poe's tale, *The Man in the Crowd* (1840). The first-person narrator reports how on an autumn evening he sits at the window of a London coffee house and observes the peculiar behaviour of an old man, behaviour so peculiar that the narrator feels compelled to leave the coffee house and follow this odd fellow for an entire night and day back and forth across London. The old man thus forces the narrator to become a reluctant *flâneur*. Finally, the narrator, exhausted by the walking, attempts to confront the old man, who refuses to make eye contact much less engage in conversation, and simply walks on. The narrator, resigned to strolling again, determines that the old man is simply a 'man in the crowd' and like a book that is impossible to read.

There was also the anti-urban tradition in English literature. It stretches from the advocates of the English province, Jane Austen and the Brontë sisters, to Thomas Hardy, whose anti-city profession for nature (*Far from the Madding Crowd*, 1874) can be read as a counter piece to Poe's narratives, and D H Lawrence, who frankly hated London. In contrast, George Orwell dared one more comparison in 1933: *Down and Out in Paris and London* is a work of impressive social analysis and moving human concern. It deals with the swallowing-up of the individual in the deserts of the city as well as the permanent idling of the *flâneur* who has long since become a hardship case.

And today? London literature is parcelling itself out. What is happening is happening in the suburbs, which we will come back to at some length later. Here is just a sample: Hanif Kureishi presented the exemplary novel on the question of the suburban world: *The Buddha of Suburbia* (1990), the story of an Indian father who suddenly decides to train for the Yoga Olympics and literally turns all his relationships and himself upside down. Martin Amis deals with the far less humorous toughness of this apparently endlessly expanding city, where the judgement is found: 'The people in here, they're like London, they're like the streets of London, a long way from any shape I've tried to equip them with, strictly non-symmetrical, exactly lopsided – far from many things, and far from art.'

In literature, London resembles a huge trap, a network of irregular systems of temptation, which encroach on the inhabitants. The reader of this literature, however, eventually learns to accommodate himself in the labyrinth of this fascinating capital city. But even the illegibility of London can be reading material, as a passage from *London Fields* (1989) demonstrates:

'There was a time when I thought I could read the streets of London. I thought I could peer into the ramps and passages, into the smoky dispositions, and make some sense of things. But now I don't think I can. Either I'm losing it, or the streets are getting harder to read. Or both. I can't read books, which are meant to be easy, easy to read. No wonder, then, that I can't read streets, which we all know to be hard – metal-lined, reinforced, massively concrete. And getting harder, tougher. Illiterate themselves, the streets are illegible. You just cannot read them any more.'

Let us delve into this labyrinth a bit more. And if in the process we search for the most sobering description of 19th-century London, then it will probably be found in Friedrich Engels' analysis in *Condition of the Working Class in England* (1845):

'A town, such as London, where a man may wander for hours together without reaching the beginning of the end, without meeting the slightest hint which could lead to the inference that there is open country within reach, is a strange thing. This colossal centralisation, this heaping together of two and a half millions of human beings at one point, has multiplied the power of this two and a half millions a hundredfold ... But the sacrifices which all this has cost become apparent later. After roaming the streets of the capital a day or two, making headway with difficulty through the human turmoil and the endless lines of vehicles, after visiting the slums of the metropolis, one realises for the first time that these Londoners have been forced to sacrifice the best qualities of their human nature, to bring to pass all the marvels of civilisation which crowd their city; that a hundred powers which slumbered within them have remained inactive, have been suppressed ... The very turmoil of the streets has something repulsive, something against which human nature rebels. The hundreds of thousands of all classes and ranks crowding past each other, are they not all human beings with the same qualities and powers, and with the same interest in being happy? ... And still they crowd by one another as though they had nothing in common, nothing to do with one another, and their only agreement is the tacit one, that each keeps to his own side of the pavement, so as not to delay the opposing streams of the crowd, while it occurs to no man to honour another with so much as a glance. The brutal indifference, the unfeeling isolation of each in his private interest, becomes the more repellent and offensive, the more these individuals are crowded together, within a limited space.'

Two and a half decades earlier Percy Bysshe Shelley created the poetic parallel to this analysis, which indirectly determines that the London cobblestones are not suited for building revolutionary barricades, in the third part of his poem, *Peter Bell*:

> *Hell is a city much like London –*
> *A populous and a smoky city;*
> *There are all sorts of people undone,*
> *And there is little or no fun done;*
> *Small justice shown, and still less pity.*

Let us press on, on our side of the pavement, to the next entrance to the Underground; for everything hellish needs depth.

London Underground

L abyrinth of labyrinths: the maze in the underworld. London's underground canals, rivers, the Underground system. Down into the
depths in a lift or on an endless escalator. For the Londoner spends a good
part of his life in this underground, in poorly-ventilated shafts, in overcrowded trains. In the summer of 2001 there was an outcry after a report
claimed that temperatures in the Underground trains had far exceeded
the levels which the European Commission had established as suitable for
the transport of livestock.

The Londoner refers to this infernal object of his enduring love-hate
relationship as 'the Tube'. A few statistics. The Tube totals 280 kilometres of track, of which one-third is subterranean. The first subterranean
line (between Paddington and Farringdon Street) was opened in 1863,
and that all-important north-south connection in London, the Northern
Line, in 1890. By 1900 London had the most modern, electrified Underground network; it has now become the most outdated, inefficient and
expensive in the so-called civilised world. On average, two despairing
people throw themselves in front of trains pulling into stations each week.
It is also statistically proven that slipping on *green* grapes is the most frequent cause of accidents on the platforms and passageways of the Underground. More frequent even, and this may be surprising, than carelessly
discarded banana skins; because rubbish bins are to be sought in vain on
the platforms: they were removed because of the threat of the IRA hiding

bombs in them, a threat that has continued from newer sources.

There can be no doubt that the Tube is a cultural centre, a social studies subject of the first rank, an experience, an emotive word, a political issue in view of its proverbially poor service. Depending on your taste, you may count on the positive side of the ledger that the Tube offers its own world of advertising. It brings forth poetry and comforts those who are combating shortage of breath and panic attacks with individually mounted poems arranged at the level of the handrail. The Tube served as an air raid shelter in the Second World War; buskers are now allowed to perform on colourful platforms, sponsored by a major brewery.

The Tube is no place for claustrophobes; any more than it is for talkative types. One can practice instantaneous assessment of people without ever exchanging a word. In the overcrowded carriage, where you come into quite close physical contact with others, not a word is ever spoken. Should the train come to an unscheduled halt in the middle of a tunnel for any length of time, you might hear an appropriately distorted voice whispering some sort of explanation over the tannoy into the sauna-like atmosphere. Anyone tempted to let loose some verbal expression of displeasure amongst these passengers, all pressed together like sardines in a tin, unmistakably reveals himself as a person of limited self-control caused by a deficient upbringing – a foreigner, in other words.

It is hopeless, of course, to keep a look out for my Lady in Yellow here. But it would be interesting to see how she would continue to read in this cramped physical torment. Everybody reads on the train, and the various reading techniques people develop on the Tube are amazing. They bury their glances in printer's ink, turn the pages skilfully, while the rattling and shaking of the train often requires acrobatic adjustments of balance in order to counter the centrifugal force. Often a page is reread several times because despite all efforts or insufficient balancing skills, it is impossible to turn the page. One's glance remains glued to this single page in order to avoid any possible eye-contact with fellow passengers. A one-centimetre gap to the next person must be preserved in all circumstances. Physical contact – even if only back-to-back – suggests something immoral. On one occasion last summer I observed (I am following my irregular diary notes here) the following incident. An innocent, overly ripe, voluptuous young London girl, with a breathtaking neckline that exposed subtly tattooed breasts for general pleasure, indignantly pulled her arm away from the man seated to her right. This visibly shy, gaunt, bespectacled grey-suiter, probably an accountant (London has the greatest density of accountants of all major cities) must have touched her with his arm. A withered anorexic-looking woman sat on the girl's left reading D H Lawrence's *Women in Love*.

The Tube. The modern Swiss writer, Adolf Muschg, tells of a relative who, whilst director of the London Swiss Centre, displayed paintings of the Swiss mountains to people seeking shelter in the tunnels during the Second World War. The display was accompanied by suggestions to visit this paradise after the end of the war. Stirring wanderlust in the midst of survival fear – Adolf Muschg's honourable relative should deserve our undying gratitude. To this day most of the posters on the Tube platforms advertise holidays to purer alternative worlds – whether Scotland, New Zealand, the Caribbean or even Switzerland.

One is also reminded, though, of Henry Moore and his drawings of the Tube as a huge air-raid shelter network in which hundreds of thousands of people found safety during the Second World War. Moore sketched people who lay wrapped like mummies in the sheltering tunnels, while above them buildings were collapsing. Moore called his drawings *Falling Buildings*, created shortly after an air raid on London. This exhibition of Moore's work from 1939–42, which I happened to come upon in the National Gallery during a day trip to Honecker's East Berlin in 1984, where there were so many reminders of the immediacy of the war, was unforgettable. I saw these drawings by Moore as fragments of a mirror, which attempted to show you that in the moment of viewing you yourself could become a terrified mummy, barely alive.

Oxford Circus Station, Platform 6, about 7:30 in the morning. This is the place to encounter Christopher Ross. He calls himself a philosopher. He earns his living currently as one of the station assistants, which

London Underground deploys at strategically important and notoriously overcrowded platforms in case of any emergency. It is possible to think more deeply, maybe even deeper on the platforms of the Tube than in your study. Christopher began his professional career as a carpet smuggler in Dubai, was next a camel driver in Australia and then had a small role as a Jesuit priest in a Japanese soap opera.

He wears an orange vest over his uniform while on duty, tests fire alarms and sweet-vending machines to ensure they are working, runs off beggars, keeps an eye out for suspicious packages and provides first aid when a passenger comes tumbling out of the oven nearly fainting. In his spare time he writes – about the Tube. His book, *Tunnel Visions* (2001), offers a philosophy born out of the London Underground. Observations of a security guard who keeps an eye on the human tide that floods past him on Platform 6 of Oxford Circus Station. His Underground philosophy originates from the question, whether we follow the tracks or whether we are (nevertheless) free. Whether we become the train and thus transport foreign freight. Whether I am my own engine or am I simply pulled along.

The underground network of any city, the netherworld of sewers, mains and pipes, is like a subtext of the metropolis. When I enter one of the lifts on the Tube that carry me down into the depths, I am reminded of the mining industry, which is dying out everywhere; I see all of us who are standing in the lift as miners, blackened with coal dust, equipped with lights, so near to a life in daylight. Shift change: Good luck! Forty metres under Tottenham Court Road we, the modern metropolitans, can touch stone from the Paleolithic era. Think about it.

What the Italian novelist Italo Svevo saw in Woolwich, the change in social class of passers-by depending on the time of day, is equally observable on the Tube. If you are sitting in the Tube at six in the morning, regardless of the line, the majority of the passengers are immigrants heading to their minimum-wage jobs in the restaurants and sandwich bars. Two hours later the same train will be full of white-collar workers heading for their offices, which the immigrants will have cleaned in the meantime. Another two hours later and tourists and idlers populate the carriages and use up the money that the previous shift will have made available to them, mostly in the form of credit.

It is time to get off. Time for more of the surface of the city. Do I know why I got off at this particular stop? Green Park. Green Park again. Always Green Park. I surface engulfed by the cloud of sweet-dusty warmth that flows out of all Underground stations, the cloud in which flowers, offered on sale in green buckets at the entrance, wilt particularly quickly. I was just re-reading in the Tube a piece by that most Anglophile of post-war German writers, who now only seems to be remembered for his ingenious book on Mozart, namely Wolfgang Hildesheimer's *Mitteilungen an Max über den Stand der Dinge und anderes* ('Notes to Max on the State of Affairs and other Issues', 1983).

Whilst reading it I felt I was sharing it with the late W G Sebald, who liked his friends to call him 'Max'. Among his important works was *Schwindel, Gefühle* ('Vertigo', 1990). In that magical work, although he usually avoided London as a theme, he also wrote of the hallucinogenic 'sweet dusty warmth' of the London Underground. I kept wanting to tell Sebald that I read Wolfgang Hildesheimer's *Mitteilungen an Max* like a letter I had written to him myself. But since 14 December 2001, the day of his fatal accident, it has been too late for that. Generally speaking, it is inevitably too late for something every day and every hour – particularly in this city, where appointments now barely have meaning because of this ever more chaotic transport infrastructure. Reliable, punctual, keepable appointments are hardly worth making anymore. Appointments have become approximations in London, rough orientation points that are treated like party jokes.

I still do not know why I got off at Green Park Station. I pass the headlines into Half Moon Street. Because of the street name. Half Moon Street runs into Curzon Street. Three times I mutter under my breath: Curzon Street. A traffic warden standing next to me, keeping an eye out for parking offenders, must have heard my mumbling and said: 'You are in Curzon Street, sir.' I thanked him and remembered: Lord and Lady Claverton in Curzon Street! Of course. Wolfgang Hildesheimer's fictitious character Andrew Marbot visited Curzon Street during his grand tour in 1820 and spent some time with his acquaintances, the Clavertons. With Lady Catherine, his mother: 'Here in London, in the Clavertons' town house in Curzon Street, in one of the upper rooms – it could only be two of them – is where it happened, the unthinkable. What had built up over the years, now erupted with full force and finally became the fulfilment of a passionate mutual adoration, in a manner that could not be more forbidden or sinful; the act of incest, an alarming fate, that could not be defended against and one which perhaps neither partner might have wanted to fight against; so they both became victims and hangman in one.'

So much for the narrator in Hildesheimer's biography of Andrew Marbot, who never existed, but who could have existed. When you see the portrait that Henry Raeburn painted of a lady in 1804, now hanging in the National Gallery of Scotland in Edinburgh, which Hildesheimer suggests is Lady Catherine Marbot, then you understand why Andrew fell for her.

Whoever leaves the Underground and its sweetly anaesthetising warmth can never be sure where he might lose himself. That is what I thought and went on my way – confused – back to the Underground, of course.

3

What Defines London

As mentioned before, London copes with an average annual population increase of 40,000. Just think: there could be another Charles Dickens amongst the new arrivals, as it was in the early autumn of 1822. Dickens was ten years old when he moved with his family from Chatham to the metropolis, which was feverish in every respect. Epidemics are rather less frequent these days than they were in Dickens' time, apart from flu epidemics which are now more likely to break out in the countryside first.

When Verdi arrived here in June 1847, he cried out: 'Chaos is London! What confusion! Paris is nothing by comparison. The people scream, the poor cry, steamers rushing past, people on horseback, in carriages, on foot and all are wailing like the damned … London is a city, unique in the world.'

What is London? Only the few neighbourhoods near Westminster? Or the amorphous mass encircled by the three-to-four-lane, but still chronically congested ring road, the M25 Motorway. Completed in 1986, it has become the standard for all matters of London traffic and orientation questions. If you live 'within the M25' then you belong to Greater London.

This M25 circular motorway is called the London Orbital. Every tailback-plagued driver feels like a satellite that creeps rather than flies around the city on this orbital. It is totally overcrowded, like the skies above London, where many planes are forced into holding patterns before they can start their descent to London's busiest airport, Heathrow. Iain Sinclair calls the M25 the metal chastity belt of the metropolis in his novel, *London Orbital* (2002). Sinclair's choice of theme is indicative. Up to now he has been known as the fictional chronicler of Whitechapel, the heart of London's East End. Now he is turning outwards to that in-between space that is becoming ever more important for most London-ers: those commuters around the M25, where it is still seething like a bit of the big city but beginning to smell of chemical fertiliser. The Thames cuts right through the M25, dividing those within the Orbital into those living either north or south of the river.

Ah – the Thames! In Dickens' day a stinking cesspool whose stench was so pungent that sessions in Parliament had to be adjourned. And indeed the path of the Thames, viewed from above or on a map, resembles a large intestine, shaped in a form suitable for the excretions of a global city. It is an unusual river, which one continually encounters with mixed feelings. The English pastoral is watered, so to speak, by the Thames upstream towards the county of Gloucestershire where it rises. One thinks of the Henley Royal Regatta, an event which has been staged since 1829, a gathering of the finest, reminiscent of days gone by with all the colourful marquees and pennants, flamboyant ladies' hats and picnic baskets. Downstream offers a different picture these days. The former warehouses with their variety of odours and dilapidation, the Docklands, have transformed themselves into a glittering, investment-grade sterile conglomeration of luxury flats and office silos. The 'true' East Enders were pushed out to the north and southeast. Pushed out; you could also say driven out by property devel-opers. And here on the bank of the river is the Millennium Dome, the symbol of gigantic miscalculation. London's post-modern folly.

The Thames – I instinctively always see her as Tissot painted her: bus-tling, full of trading vessels, though with enough room for pleasure craft. Or as Turner, Whistler or Monet perceived her: deserted, empty, shrouded in smoke and fog; or colourful like a painting by Derain. Or almost myth-ical like the consistently under-valued William Alistair Macdonald, who painted the timber wharves of London around 1900 and an incomparable *View from Blackfriars Bridge* looking upstream.

The Thames has comparatively little behind her when she flows into the sea at Southend, and at the same time a lot. She? Was there not an Old Father Thames to whom Raffaelle Monti created a monument, which could be seen at the Great Exhibition in London's Crystal Palace and can still be admired at Lechlade? The swans of the Thames are under royal protection; Richard the Lionheart is supposed to have set the first ones out on the river. And there is still a Royal Swan Keeper, who is responsible for all the swans on the Thames. And do we not still float in Jerome K Jerome's proverbial Thames boat with the three men and their dog?

If the Thames was once an intestine and at the same time the main artery of London, then it is now only a branch of the primary transport stream. Thus, contemporary London literature bypasses it, leaving it on the side. But this river is worthy of a great elegy; after all 51 passengers on the pleasure boat *Marchioness* drowned here off Southwark when she collided with the dredger *Bowbelle*, under circumstances that have still not completely been explained.

Ah, London. Whoever attempts to describe this city must necessarily be entered in the Grey Book of Failure. For words cannot but fail to describe this undulating city. The German dramatist Friedrich Hebbel excused his failure to develop a coherent text about London in a letter to his wife in June 1862: 'And London? I can no more describe it for you than I could a rainbow and the Falls of the Rhine. Not that I feel overwhelmed, my nature is capable of coping with large dimensions and multiplications do not impress me for long, but in the end everything leads to multiplications. It is too much on its own, one object squeezes another, the pen sways and the hand goes lame. The most lasting impression is the moral climate which, like the physical, rules every breath, the free movement of the people within the constraints of lawfulness with one word: the respect it has of itself.'

He lived in Finsbury Park, visited Joseph Paxton's Crystal Palace, the City, Westminster, Richmond and Belsize Park. What he missed was the middle ground in the cityscape: 'I get seasick on solid ground with this horrible noise about nothing. In the final instance there is nothing behind anything except the empty fist that wants money and more money and even more money.' Here there were the demonstratively wealthy, who according to Hebbel, would throw £1,000 into the Thames out of sheer high spirits and then again there was in 'side streets the cruellest squalor, not even hidden and pushed into the corners, as elsewhere, but out in the open'.

When he returned to Paris at the end of June 1862, he drew breath: 'I felt as though put through a mill in London; it is impossible to think during the day or sleep in the night ... If you know Hamburg, you have the key to the metropolis of Great Britain, except that the German city is to the English one as a chalk sketch is to a completed painting; during the week crassest egotism in its most brutal form and on Sundays an even more horrible feeding of the conscience and morale through the most repulsive Puritanism.' Hebbel's project to create an 'overview' of the Thames metropolis failed because he not only observed the exterior of London, but saw through it into its blackest depths. And what he saw left him speechless.

The other failure carried the working title *London Town*. Henry James attempted it between 1907 and 1909. He had signed a contract with Macmillan four years earlier and purchased a notebook with 140 pages for this purpose. But he only filled 36 of them with fragmentary notes. They are set up like a diary, which leads you to believe that Henry James may have considered presenting his London observations in diary form. He searched for the old London (like Dickens before him) and only found, as he noted, the 'hideous Tower Bridge', which he denounced as historical kitsch. He was on the trail of *his* Southwark, the Southwark of Shakespeare's time, and only found ugly workhouses and factories. James, who was accustomed to the elite clubs in Pall Mall and Carlton Terrace, was frightened by the social realities of London, to which he was sporadically exposed while riding in a well-upholstered cab. He had lived in London for 20 years, but what he was able to see on his brief outings into that 'other London' left him, that cosmopolitan writer from New York, mute.

One so wanted to be like Voltaire, who arrived in London, as he emphasised, in *lovely* and nothing but lovely weather, having fled that most absolute dungeon named France, believing himself to breathe nothing but freedom and being handed from banquet to reception. Voltaire sensed something about the essence of Londoners though, when he experienced the following event in a small circle of friends. In the midst of a conversation another friend joined them and announced with an 'unmoving face' as follows:

> '"Molly cut her throat this morning. Her lover found her dead with a shearing knife next to her in her room." This Molly was a pretty and very rich young woman, who was about to marry the same man who found her dead. The gentlemen, who were all Molly's friends, heard the news without batting an eyelash. Only one of them inquired what happened to her lover; "he bought the shearing knife", someone in the company replied coldly.
>
> 'Horrified by such an unusual death and by the indifference of these gentlemen, I could not avoid inquiring what reason could have driven such an apparently happy young lady to take her own life in such a gruesome manner; I was simply given the answer that the east wind was blowing.'

In a book about London an east wind is always blowing, which makes the people here unpredictable, as does the *fön*, *scirocco* or *mistral* in other places. Because a book about London cannot be planned. It basically consists only of chapter titles, which it would be hubris to trade in. Let us go a few miles into the east wind, to Southwark, there where everything in literary London begins.

Where am I here? In a square. Is it Fitzroy or Tavistock? And there she is again, the Lady in Yellow, looking somewhat paler, faceless almost, and yet of alienating beauty. She is reading, slowly going round the Square. Perhaps she is absorbed by pages that tell her how to square the magic circles of London.

Diversion II

The Green In The Square

Where residents once let their cattle graze, they now have their benches. Entry (to the private garden squares) for keyholders only.

Each London square has its own green flair. The more elegant it is, the more lush and varied in vegetation the green space in its centre will be. Sometimes it is planted in an ellipse, sometimes a rectangle, but it is always surrounded by an asphalt ring of road and pavement, which serves as approach and parking zone for its residents. The square is a park in a cutaway and as such the matrix of the Thames metropolis, at least of its inner districts.

Some of the squares, with their solid railings and old trees, are only accessible to the squares' residents, especially when the homes surrounding it belong to the wealthy neighbourhoods. It is counted as one of the greatest privileges to have a key to this green pleasure.

The green of these park-like pseudo-gardens feeds an illusion: that nature exists in a harmonious relationship with the city, that this nature, a piece of the much lauded rural pastoral, could be brought into the city without detriment and that each square could compete with the great parks of the city. Likewise, each Square creates the illusion that there could be such a thing as public intimacy and an intimate public. The green space of a square, inaccessible to non-residents, resembles an intimate 'no go' zone in reality, where the obligatory wrought-iron fencing represents a form of chastity belt. The green in the midst of the houses is an apparently fertile oasis in the stone desert, a world of stone, which of course in the case of squares insists on extreme elegance and refined civility. The afore-mentioned Karl Philipp Moritz was one of the first visitors who, in 1782, commented on the architectural significance of the square, implying that it structured the newer parts of London, literally giving them shape.

Take for instance Onslow Square, created by C J Freake in South Kensington in 1846. I mention it also because Robert Fitzroy lived in one of the richly stuccoed interiors. He was captain of HMS *Beagle*, in which Charles Darwin sailed to the Galapagos Islands. Fitzroy, in turn, brought back a few Galapagos plants and set them out in the square garden where they promptly withered, but as good plant spirits they protect their siblings of more resistant varieties. Fitzroy, who lived at Number 38, committed suicide in the Square, apparently in despair over the idea that his voyages may have assisted Darwin in challenging the authority of the Bible.

Little is known about the garden designers of the squares. It is known, however, that a certain Humphry Repton made his name in 1800 with the design of the green space in Russell Square. He envisioned three fountains that would alternate in the rise and fall of their water jets. Popular belief claims this rhythm flowed continuously until 18 June 1815, the date of the Battle of Waterloo.

Then there were squares that had no greenery at all initially, Hanover Square for example. This square was fenced off, but its centre was bare. Treeless, gaplessly paved and built on: around 1780 the elegant residents of Hanover Square still believed green was vulgar and not city-like. Hanover Square had something of a large music salon about it, ever ready to take up the magical sounds that Johann Christian, the 'London' Bach, Haydn, Paganini and Liszt created in the Hanover Square Rooms, and to give them a over-dimensional space for resonance that was not to be dampened by any green bits.

Not so Leicester Square, whose seemingly modest green zone belies the fact that it was originally protected by decree to allow the residents to lay out their laundry to dry on the bushes and graze their cattle. After

1808 the centre of Leicester Square ran to seed. The condition of this space appeared to be a hot topic of debate and vexation, and rumours ran rampant: in the green wilderness of Leicester Square, as several London gazettes were still conjecturing around 1855, the 'unwashed Street Arabs of Westminster' romped about, doing un-Christian things with stray dogs and cats under cover of the bushes. In the end, in the 1870s, Disraeli's government had to deal with the green eyesore at the heart of the Empire. It was decided to restore the space to its original condition and that meant, as in the time of Charles II, replanting a number of elm trees.

The example of Leicester Square gives rise to a vision of botanical horror: the undergrowth of a neglected square gains the upper hand, extends to the buildings all around; its roots undermine the foundations, the ground rises, the walls spilt, and the houses are pushed apart. The square spreads and regally takes the place of houseplants, and finally the residents. That would be the reverse of what happened in Montagu Square at the end of the 19th century: the residents had their houseplants brought into the centre of the square in order to demonstrate that this area was part of their communal living space. After all, even the generously spacious Bedford Square was not accessible to the general public until 1893. The green reservoir was often more stubbornly defended than access to the royal parks.

How then does this square-green distinguish itself from the great parks of London? On the one hand, it is carefully surrounded by buildings, a small reminder of nature, a green lung, pseudo-natural oxygen tent, a simulation of an oasis. On the other hand it is a privilege in green, an exclusive piece of vegetation (the major exception being the public greens of Russell Square and Gordon Square) and a controlled organic memorial to the fields of yesteryear. Yet, one could also see something entirely different in this square-green: the aesthetically successful paradox of a squared circle. Because that is exactly what the square is. A token and ideal model for the mutual domestication and ultimate reconciliation of nature and city.

4

Southwark, or where Late Modernism Builds on Primitive Rocks

'Send a philosopher to London; please God no poet!', Heinrich Heine called out in Cheapside, where he observed the 'human tides surging' around him, and from whom there was more to learn than from all the books at the Leipzig Fair. He had stationed himself on a corner to watch the hustle and bustle in what had been the main market place of medieval London (*ceap* or *chepe* is the old English word for market). Heine considered an ability to read the city and its people as the measure of true learning in London. A 'philosopher' would see, Heine continued, the Holy Ghost drifting above this human tide and the 'deepest secrets of the social order would reveal themselves to him suddenly'. Cheapside as the heartbeat of the world.

What a (social) philosopher might fathom would remain, according to Heine, hidden to a simple poet, even a German romantic. For the 'absolute seriousness of all matters, this colossal uniformity, these machine-like movements, this moroseness of joy itself, this exaggerated London suffocates the imagination and rends the heart.'

Heine stood at a corner of Cheapside as a poet inclined towards social philosophy. Like Hebbel after him, he saw through the city and its unconscious, mechanical streaming, its constant living above its means. John Bull, Heine wrote, overexerts his brain day and night to invent new machines to the point of self-martyrdom, 'and he sits and calculates by the sweat of his brow, and hurries and runs, without looking about much, from the harbour to the Exchange, from the Exchange to the Strand' and in his hurry and haste runs into the 'poor German poet' who is gaping at a picture gallery on the corner of Cheapside, with an irate, 'God damn!'. But what was this poet staring at in this gallery's display? A painting of 'The French Crossing the Beresina': Napoleon's retreat after the disaster of the Russian campaign.

Napoleon in London – that would have been *the* thing for Heine: that genius on the island of mediocrity. But he, Heine the poet, was there himself now, instead of his idolised martyr of St Helena. Heine's harsh critique of London can be explained by his repugnance to those English politicians who destroyed *his* Napoleon. He considered Wellington a bad joke, and Sir Walter Scott only a tired ex-poet in view of his feeble biography of Napoleon.

A few years after Napoleon's death (Heine called it 'murder'), the German poet went to England to see with his own eyes the capital of this country, which had desecrated his God of freedom. He experienced the emancipation of Catholics, although he remained deliberately silent on Wellington's major role in this reform. He generally compared it with Napoleon's emancipation of the Jews, which the very young Heine had experienced while living in Düsseldorf when it was under French occupation. For Heine, Napoleon was the creator of the *Code Civil*, through which he achieved a level of legitimacy in the eyes of the poet that other crowned heads of state, including the Hanoverians on the Thames, could only dream of.

Still standing on the corner of Cheapside, Heine called himself to order after this digression; and now, at second glance, the roar and tumult of the crowd in Cheapside and in London generally is like one great Beresina bridge, 'where everyone tries to squeeze through, eking out a little bit of existence in insane fear.'

It seems to me that Heine may have had his philosophical considerations on a corner across from Ironmonger Lane. Incidentally, this is where the house stood in which in 1816 the young John Keats worked on his first poetry volume, published a year later under the simplest of all titles, *Poems*. They were poems that with every word and every verse attempted to drive away the rough reality of the city and the screaming and dying in Guy's Hospital where he had assisted since 1815. Heine knew nothing of that when he stood and stood and was amazed with revulsion as he saw through the urban insanity. It should come as no surprise that he eventually sought out the insane asylum of Bedlam and there encountered real philosophers.

Heine, that analytically observant man on the corner of Cheapside, commented: 'These brick houses become the same colour due to the damp air and soot, namely brownish olive green; they are all built in the same style, usually two or three windows wide, three high, and decorated with small red chimneys on top that look like bloody teeth that have been pulled, set such that the broad, regular streets which they form appear to be just two endless barracks-like houses. This probably has its purpose under the circumstances that every English family, even couples without children, wants to live in their own house, their own castle, and rich investors accommodating such a need build entire streets in which they sell off the houses one at a time.'

Heine described a society in which everyone wanted ownership, even if the poor owner possessed only squalor. And he saw the West End with its uniformity of riches that stared at him everywhere. The stranger who 'wanders through the major streets of London', Heine continued, 'and who does not happen upon the actual rabble neighbourhood, sees nothing or very little of the tremendous squalor that is present in London.' Because the squalor had been pushed into the dark, damp alleys where infants were dying of hunger at the slack breasts of their emaciated mothers.

Heine never made it across Southwark Bridge, which the famous bridge builder, John Rennie, replaced with a massive cast-iron construction between 1814 and 1819, to the oldest part of London. Its Roman origin was only discovered seven years after his visit. More recently Norman Foster built a bridge across the Thames in the vicinity of Southwark, over to Tate Modern; it turned out to be a wobbly bridge that had to be closed for a year.

No, Heine did not get as far as Southwark. What happened in a high gothic room next to St Mary's Church – 'in the Monthe of Maii' – remained hidden from him: Sir John Gower, one of England's great poets, a close friend of Geoffrey Chaucer, composed his first English verses. Until that time he had only written in French and Latin.

What Gower wrote was recited or sung in public; Chaucer, on the other hand, wrote for silent reading. The prologue to the pilgrimage in the *Canterbury Tales*, written for contemplative hours, has its beginning here in Southwark. Southwark – it is London's primeval origin in terms of city development as well as in the poetic sense. The early greats of English literature are gathered at Southwark Cathedral, now freed of soot and smog residue, a gleaming greyish white as if newly built. You can walk past them: Lancelot Andrewes, whom T S Eliot immortalised in a remarkable essay about the modernity of clerical poetry, next to John Gower; John Donne and the great Shakespeare's brother Edmund who in 1599 helped to establish the Globe Theatre, the now restored jewel of Southwark. Between the new Tate Modern Gallery, this power plant of modernity, and the Globe Theatre I suddenly discovered her again: my Lady in Yellow. She surfaced in the surging crowd on Riverside Walk, still clad primarily in yellow, but with a black cape. She is reading whilst walking in the direction of the Globe, reading what will *not* be staged there today, *cannot* be staged there. I think I can make out at this distance that she is reading *The Pickwick Papers*, perhaps the chapter in which the 'White Hart' appears, the same pub which also plays a minor role in Shakespeare's *Henry VI*. I could tell my Lady in Yellow, moreover, that this is where the 'Queen's Head' stood. It was once owned by a certain John Harvard who then sold it and used the proceeds to found a university near Boston in New England simply named after himself. Would that be going too far? Nothing can go too far in a city like this.

So, into the Globe. *King Lear* is playing. Turn off mobile 'phones; we're going back into the Elizabethan age. 'Beat at this gate, that let thy folly in, and thy dear judgement out!' The scent of fresh sawdust is in the air. The Lady in Yellow has managed to get a seat; I am standing in the pit.

She is reading her book; it cannot be *Lear*, but more likely as said *The Pickwick Papers* (or is it *Vanity Fair* (1847–8) by Thackeray – both pocket editions have these obscene George Cruikshank caricatures of contemporaries; Cruikshank who published these unsurpassed satirical drawings of the notorious Southwark waterworks that made a fortune with untreated dirty water from the Thames). She is certainly not studying *Lear*, that is for certain, but continues to read in her massive book and only puts it aside at the very end when the insane Lear staggers lost across the sawdust heath with the dead Cordelia in his arms. And when at the end, the Duke of Albany calls out: 'The oldest hath borne most; we that are young Shall never see so much, nor live so long' and a storm of applause erupts around me, my Lady in Yellow carries on calmly reading. And the feeling creeps over me that perhaps she gained more from this performance than I did.

Southwark has always seethed. Since 1462 there had been an annual three-day fair in September, which was only banned in Handel's day (1743) because of the 'excessive number of pickpockets and prostitutes'. London's great diarists of the 17th century, Samuel Pepys and John Evelyn, did not miss out on the spectacle. In 1660, Evelyn noted the irresistible sight of an Italian tightrope walker and trained monkeys who were able to dance with burning candles on their heads and baskets full of eggs, without breaking a single one. Pepys was less enthusiastic about these festivities eight years later as the dirt on the streets must have been outrageous. Ten years before the Southwark Fair was closed down, the wild, popular counterpart to the refined Vauxhall Gardens in which *concerti grossi* were performed, William Hogarth captured in an engraving what made this festivity so unmistakeable: tightly-packed crowds, both improvised and stage-managed performances of every kind, above all pleasure in the chaos.

Back into the City, across Southwark Bridge, past Cheapside again, Heine has left his corner post, into this labyrinth.

5

The City – the Heart of which World?

It is three o'clock in the morning on 2 September 1666. The housekeeper of the Clerk of the Acts to the Navy Board, Samuel Pepys, Fellow of the Royal Society, reports a tremendous fire in the City. In his dressing gown, the great diarist looks for himself from the window in the upper storey of his house in Seething Lane near the Tower of London: 'but, being unused to such fires as followed, I thought it far enough off, and so went to bed again, and to sleep...'.

If one wants to learn something of English imperturbability, then one should digest this sentence with its unsurpassable casualness, which captures it to a 't'. Toward seven a.m. Pepys glanced again at the fire, 'so to my closett to set things to rights after yesterday's cleaning'. Just 24 hours later and Pepys had to evacuate his house in the face of the conflagration that was now threatening Seething Lane, moving his gold and his wife (in that order) to safety. Later it would turn out that his house was one of the few in the area spared by the flames.

What Pepys wrote in his diary in those September days became an early masterpiece of literary realism. Pepys was practised in realism, as one year earlier he had reported on the plague, which raged in London between 1664 and 1665 and claimed an estimated 100,000 victims. Those were times of extreme climatic variations. In February 1665, Pepys experiences one of the 'coldest days, all say, they ever felt in England ...' with the Thames frozen and 'birds freezing to death in mid-flight', where as

May brought record high temperatures and continued the spread of the plague. Thousands of Londoners lived on small boats on the river in order to flee the epidemic. And literature developed on the street, for example in the form of a children's rhyme. To this day, children sing: 'Ring-a-ring 'roses/ A pocket full of posies' A-tishoo! A-tishoo!/ We all fall down.' In the vernacular, 'roses' referred to the pink skin rash that was one of the first symptoms of the plague. A pocket full of 'posies', were the sweet aromatic herbs that one carried in order to be able to stand the smell of decomposing bodies. The handkerchief refers to the sneezing that indicated the plague patient was in the final stages of the illness. And then the deadly finale: 'We all fall down.' At one point, Pepys writes that he found his 'coachman to drive easily and easily, at last stood still, and come down hardly able to stand' suddenly feeling very ill, already marked by death. And a few months after the plague, the Great Fire, all this whilst the country was at war with the Dutch.

As the plague carried off the people, so the fire destroyed their possessions, although 'only' nine inhabitants are claimed to have died in the fire. Pepys transformed this horror into the medium of literature, a horror that he described from two perspectives. On the one hand he wrote as the sovereign's observer who in order to obtain an overview had climbed a church tower to gain a panoramic view of the extent of the devastation and then reported to the King at Whitehall, while on the other hand he wrote from the view of a terrified near-victim, worried for his possessions.

'The Great Fire' – one should have the crackling of its flames in one's ear when one wanders through the labyrinth of the City, coming from Fleet Street, past the former headquarters of *The Daily Telegraph*, the building which Michael Frayn labelled an imperial monstrosity which looked more like the 'Tomb of the Unknown Columnist' in his amusing Fleet Street novel, *Towards the End of the Morning* (1967). You can hear the crackling of this fire, which probably marks the most important turning point in London's history, an inferno that was exceeded only by the Blitz in the Second World War. Because after this 'Great Fire' which destroyed 87 churches, 50 livery halls and more than 14,000 houses, the decision was made to build an entirely new City rather than to reconstruct the old.

A new era began in London's reckoning of time in 1666. Sir Christopher Wren, England's greatest master builder of his time, and John Evelyn conceived a new city based on Italian precepts, without any constrictions, with broad streets and large plazas as well as spacious buildings. What this meant to Wren can be seen in St Paul's Cathedral. What they intended was a 'catholic solution' for the building of the City, an all-encompassing city building plan, generous, imaginative, open, totally in accordance with the style of the ruling Stuarts. Charles II was well aware of the prize he had in Wren. Not so the gentlemen of the City. They dreaded such plans. The fire may have destroyed the old City, but not the mercantile spirit. And this was what they wanted to defend against the 'Italian' luxury concept offered by Wren and Evelyn. The City Fathers decided on the reconstruction of the spires and trading houses, the tight proximity of clergy and commerce, the intimate communications of buyers and sellers. The City was rebuilt – pettiness on a grand scale, though more with stone than timber, but with unchanged narrowing streets and a labyrinthine maze. The City that rose again extended an invitation to become caught in the net of commerce.

What happened to the west of the City was a matter for the nobility and the developing middle classes; let them settle there, between Covent Garden and Westminster, Piccadilly and Whitehall, the Montagues and Downings, the Hitchingbrookes and Pickerings, courtiers and artists, spendthrifts all, who had no understanding of skills and trade. In the City, one always thought commercially, as befitted one's role, and eventually persuaded Parliament to finance the reconstruction between Cheapside and the Tower, London Wall and Blackfriars, with a coal tax.

For a long time, the 'Great Fire' was thought to have been a purely political attack by the French and Papists, a rumour that was rife among the homeless of the City in their camps in the west of London. In fact, it was an apparently quite apolitical French baker's apprentice by the name of Robert Hubert who supposedly after an argument with his English master baker set fire to the bakery on the night of 2 September, whereupon

41

the fire spread devastatingly quickly. He was hanged, which contemporaries held to be a remarkably mild punishment for what he had done.

If one wants to get a sense of what a house in the City during the days of the Great Fire was like, one should go from the 'Fountain Tavern' with its Pepys Memorial Room along Fleet Street to the most literary public house of Old London, 'Ye Olde Cheshire Cheese'. This is where they all came and went: Samuel Johnson who lived around the corner in Gough Square, later Charles Dickens, Alfred Tennyson, Queen Victoria's favourite poet, Mark Twain, Arthur Conan Doyle and G K Chesterton. It was also here that the members of the 'Rhymers Club', a rhyming poets' association which counted the young Irish poet William Butler Yeats amongst its members, met in the last decade of the 19th century.

Coffee houses were found in the western end of London, beginning at Covent Garden. But here in Fleet Street the primeval character with its tight spiral staircases, polished tables and decidedly uncomfortable chairs still reigned. This is where an enduring urban literature developed, without refinement.

The pub opened its doors one year after the Great Fire in a building, by the way, that also escaped the flames. Its name also had an agenda, just like the conservative rebuilding plans for the City: tried and true Cheshire cheese versus the culinary experiments of the despised Catholic Continentals. The puritan motto applied to the City, too: one eats to live and not the other way around. And for that Cheshire cheese, a tankard of ale, along with a language seasoned with a few ribald words are sufficient. That this could generate poetry in prose was to be proven in particular by Dickens with his great city novels.

How dark it is in the 'Cheshire Cheese' with its numerous small public rooms spread over two storeys, a house that in itself is a vertical labyrinth. Creaking stairs, sawdust-strewn floorboards. Though they have a daily menu, there is no daytime. It is always equally gloomy in the 'Cheshire Cheese'. My Lady in Yellow would be useful in her luminous clothes; she would be a point of light. And although nothing indicates that she might be here, I involuntarily look for her here, though in vain.

Instead, I should have searched for her at 17 Gough, or as Samuel Johnson wrote, Goff Square. This is where she had been, just before I myself entered this jewel of a Georgian townhouse where Johnson developed his extraordinary *Dictionary of the English Language* with his six assistants in 1746. I enquired of the knitting attendant whether she had seen a middle-aged woman in a yellow dress. 'And how', she answered without interrupting her knitting. She looked *very* yellow. Dazzlingly yellow. But she was only interested in the cast-iron cat which represented Hodge, Dr Johnson's favourite cat whom he idolised and to whom he would read from his dictionary. Dr Johnson also discussed controversial etymological questions with Hodge, his cat, the attendant said, while continuing to knit. The woman in yellow already knew all that, as she was given to understand at the end of her explanations about Dr Johnson's cat, which disappointed the unremitting knitter. I should go up into the Dictionary Room. And soon I was standing in front of the first edition and felt like Hodge the cat. Try to imagine Johnson, Samuel Johnson, known only as Dr Johnson in English, this linguistic genius, once the first man of letters in the country, ending up in debtors' prison in 1758, only to be bailed out for six guineas by the novelist Samuel Richardson.

Fleet Street. One tries to understand what went on here over a good 300 years: the closest possible twinning of journalism and literature. Dr Johnson founded a magazine, *The Rambler,* almost as a matter of course after finishing his nine-year effort on the *Dictionary,* presumably not without consulting Hodge, his 'owl on four legs', as he used to say. *The Rambler*, a word for climbing roses and wanderers and for one who speaks incoherently. 'To ramble on' means to speak continuously in an unstructured manner. Johnson managed to survive this journalistic babbling for two years; he wrote all the articles himself, as did Kleist later for the *Berliner Abendblätter* and Karl Kraus for *Die Fackel*. Fleet Street was one long marketplace for news in which Charles Dickens felt at home; this is where he delivered his work for the *Monthly Magazine*, this greatest journalist amongst the greatest authors like George Bernard Shaw, George Orwell and in our time, Philip Hensher.

You should allow yourself to drift through this din of the City, through which couriers sprint on their racing bikes through barely discernible gaps in the traffic in the midst of the throng, naturally equipped with breathing masks as is one or the other traffic policeman or passer-by. You could make a pilgrimage from one church to another; there were almost 100 of them before 1666. Christopher Wren alone constructed 51 new churches after the Great Fire. And all this in one square mile. There are 38 still standing, houses of God rebuilt after the destruction of German air attacks within the boundaries of the former City, each one of them a small miracle – especially today for the many homeless people who seek shelter in them.

The density of churches in the City is a phenomenon that is found nowhere else. Does it mirror the bad conscience of the financial magnates of yore? In part perhaps. But the opposite was also true. The Church saw itself at the heart of commerce; it emphasised its accumulated presence in the profane. Furthermore, these churches supported schools in the tightest space in the respective parishes. Because until the end of the 19th century people also *lived* in the City and required the opportunity to attend services on their doorstep if at all possible. (Today the City has barely 6,000 residents.) Dickens recognised this structural change and its concomitant socio-cultural impoverishment of the City, always gaining in other types of wealth. In his writings one can find descriptions how even those moved out of the City into the surrounding areas in the 1850s continued to attend services in their former City church every Sunday.

If you allow yourself to drift from St Lawrence Jewry to St Margaret Lothbury and St Stephen Walbrook, you can easily lose your sense of direction. You had intended to seek out Lombard Street, not the Stock Exchange, not Bishopsgate where Ian Fleming, the creator of James Bond, worked as a stockbroker, but the Lombard Street where Alexander Pope was born amidst the banks. Maria Beadnell, a banker's daughter and Charles Dickens' first great love, lived at No 2 Lombard Street. Love drove the 18-year-old all the way here day after day, if only to look up at the window of his beloved. For this yearning glimpse of a window he walked the entire way from Westminster and back. Maria Beadnell became Dora

Spenlow in *David Copperfield* (1849–50); David is in her thrall, wants to marry her, but he has to acknowledge that this child/woman is not a suitable match for him.

Maria Beadnell makes another appearance in a work by Dickens, this time in the form of Flora Finching in his novel *Little Dorrit* (1857). Dickens allows his protagonist, Arthur Clennam, to experience exactly his own disappointment. Twenty years after meeting Maria Beadnell she wrote him a letter. Dickens' curiosity was piqued; they met again, much to the shock of the famous author. Because sitting opposite him was an obese, perpetually giggling caricature contorted by ugliness, which appalled him. In the novel *Little Dorrit* there is a very similar meeting, except that Arthur Clennam falls into a self-destructive melancholy as a result of this profoundly disappointing confrontation with the former blossom of his youth, Flora Finching. He is sitting in a coffee house on Ludgate Hill on a grey Sunday afternoon, the deafening ringing of the City church bells in his ears and the grey vision of an empty life ahead of him.

Walter Benjamin made the observation that the urban writers of the 19th and early 20th century attempted to give the city and everything urban its own language. However, if you walk through London or any other late modern metropolis and are paying attention, you are more likely to get the impression that you are in the process of discovering the various languages of the city at each corner, whilst yourself being threatened with speechlessness in the face of this polyglot wealth. Because it is quite possible to encounter five different languages in the space of ten steps on the streets of London.

But sometimes I roam through this or that neighbourhood and get a completely different feeling. You can walk through London and believe you can feel a future tremor, which you cannot quite define, under your feet. You walk as if in a vibrating room or a ceaselessly revolving panorama. Or you believe yourself to be on a delicately balanced patchwork quilt of cultures. It would be frivolous to attempt to identify yourself with any one of them, to attempt to drop an anchor in it. You can dip into everything and anything in this urban amalgam briefly, for the duration of a Chinese, Malaysian, Bengali or Polish meal, and continue on to the next coincidence.

I actually wanted to go towards Covent Garden, but instead I seem to be approaching Whitechapel and thus the East End. Was I thinking of my Lady in Yellow again? Yes. Always. This faceless acquaintance. It seems to me as if she would take on the appearance of each of the characters or topics she was just reading about. Engrossed in *Little Dorrit*, she is like Little Dorrit. Quietly reciting *King Lear*, she has no other choice but to become Cordelia. And browsing in Johnson's dictionary, she would become its yellow cover. Beauty, thy name is metamorphosis.

And here in Whitechapel? I must not meet her here. I must not even imagine her here, my Lady in Yellow. For here she would have no other choice than to take on the appearance of Martha Turner, Annie Chapman or Mary Kelly, to mention only a few of Jack the Ripper's victims, as they appear in Marie Belloc Lowndes' play *The Lodger* (1913), which Alfred Hitchcock was to turn into a film. No, not in Whitechapel where Jack London, dressed as a penniless, down-at-heel American, had a taxi drop him off somewhere in the summer of 1902, so he could gather literary material amongst the workers and beggars; material which would later find expression in his novel, *The People of the Abyss* (1903). His example was followed by George Orwell, who one day, shortly before Christmas 1931, appeared as a rampaging drunkard because he wanted to be arrested by the police. The result of this experience is found in the novel, *1984* (1949), when Winston Smith is waiting for his interrogation in his cell, which is so foul-smelling that he nearly passes out. No, I could not do that to my Lady in Yellow. All of them have roamed through this East End. Even in the last year of his life, Dickens returned here, more specifically to Limehouse, to absorb the atmosphere that he needed for the beginning of his unfinished last novel, *The Mystery of Edwin Drood* (1870), the opium hell of the Ratcliffe Highway.

Whitechapel with its innumerable dark spots and tough shadows. Shadows of squalor. Scars of poverty. Where today primarily Bengali immigrants strive for survival, Sephardic Jews from eastern Europe had settled since the 17th century; Huguenot silk-weavers arrived here from France after 1685; the Irish followed; many Germans. Everything was suitable for trading – particularly haberdashery and second-hand clothes. It is the world of homeless shelters, workhouses and soup kitchens. Until the 1980s it was still open, that 'soup kitchen for poor Jews', founded in 1902, whose atmosphere was described by Israel Zangwill in his novel, *Children of the Ghetto* (1892). There is something peculiar about remembering that Lenin and the young Stalin lived in one of these homeless shelters in Fieldgate Street when they visited the fifth Party Conference of Russian Socialists that convened in Fulbourne Street in 1907.

However, let us examine what *the* poet of the East End, Isaac Rosenberg (1890–1918) had to say about his world in the *Ballad of Whitechapel*, which cannot be found in English schoolbooks:

> *I watched the gleams*
> *Of jagged warm lights on shrunk faces pale.*
> *I heard mad laughter as one hears in dreams,*
> *Or Hell's harsh lurid tale.*

> *The traffic rolled,*
> *A gliding chaos populous of din.*
> *A streaming wail at doom the Lord had scrawled*
> *For perilous loads of sin.*

Walking and seeing and hearing: what the stones attest to, the condemned houses speak of, what grows on the grass. Peter Ackroyd, in *Hawksmoor* (1985), told the story of Nicholas Dyer, who appears to escape this world when he builds a church but then dedicates it to Satan. He actually seems to have been at home here, the demon of the city that Milton suspected. Today you can see from here the colossal glass tower of Canary Wharf, which Ian Sinclair, one of the important contemporary British authors, calls the building that comes closest to 'the hand of God'. You could also call it a monument to Mammon or a memorial column to the idol Progress with its pyramid-shaped roof winking at aeroplanes.

When you see these glass structures that were built in the area around Wapping and the Isle of Dogs on the remains of past squalor, they appear empty, because on this scale of architecture people become a rumour, in any event barely visible but sometimes also highly-paid walk-on players. In general this is one of the remarkable characteristics of London, the contradiction between the hopelessly overpopulated metropolis and its numerous empty, speculative building developments. Poverty has been banished from these areas and a spiritual poverty has moved into the glass walls drowned in alcohol after hours.

Until the middle of the 19th century Wapping was a proverbial slum where short work was made of executing pirates. When the German writer and journalist Theodor Fontane reported on this twilight area to the east of the Tower, it had already been cleaned up a bit, and was almost cheerful; here one could live and prattle on in the coarsest manner; sailors and upright shipwrights, but also black marketeers, scoundrels, wastrels and prostitutes could be seen here. Fontane quoted Admiral Nelson, which he liked to do frequently, along the lines of: 'What do you mean riff-raff? This is the riff-raff with which I won England's battles.' If you look at Wapping today, this gleaming hothouse of speculators, then you are tempted to modify another phrase of Fontane's: 'The step from poverty to crime, which once occurred here a 1,000 times, continues today in the direction of criminal riches.'

It would be easy to allow yourself to drift down river now; the green hill of Greenwich would greet you, the Observatory that almost became the target of a bomb attack in Joseph Conrad's novel, *The Secret Agent* (1907). A dinner was given here in 1861 for Mary Ann Evans, alias George Eliot, in honour of the publication of her novel, *Silas Marner* (1861). She was the only woman present as Victorian morality dictated that society ladies should avoid the presence of a 'fallen woman' (which she was considered to be).

Blackheath would be close by, where you can sense a breeze of sea air. In Victorian times there were numerous schools here, both the superb and notorious (in one of them there were supposed to have been teachers who were themselves illiterate). Benjamin Disraeli went to one of the better schools on Blackheath; but Dickens' David Copperfield saw his school days 'on the black heath' as an exile and punishment for having bitten his stepfather.

Past Blackheath, Woolwich, where from the time of Henry VIII until 1869 warships were built. This was where the armoury of the Empire stood, but also one of the most important stoneware factories, which put its production through extreme durability tests: cups and saucers were not meant to crack when dropped onto a cabin deck from a height of two metres. And cannon balls were cast right next door. The young Henry James was fascinated by this place; Italo Svevo came here, too, when he visited London in 1901 and noted down his memories 12 years later. He came from Blackheath, where he observed that the wealth of the inhabitants stood in the way of public transport like trams and buses. Only private carriages were allowed here in this airy idyll. Svevo, who suffered from homesickness for Trieste whilst in London, noted that the main street in Woolwich, Church Lane, experienced a regular change of shifts: 'At six in the morning workers flock into it on their way to the factories or to Woolwich Dockyard (a naval shipyard). Then come the clerks on their way to the City. During the day ladies and gentlemen arrive from Blackheath too, because Charlton station, closer to their homes than Blackheath's, is convenient for them. In the evening the clerks arrive from the City and ladies and gentlemen leave for the theatre.' Yes, one would drift downstream like this, perhaps boarding a train to Rochester in Kent, making a pilgrimage to Gad's Hill where Dickens wrote about this metropolis and died, far away from the city.

But enough; back into the ventricles of the city. Because it does not have just one heart. Every part of the city is one of its hearts; and each has its very own labyrinth.

Diversion III

Nocturnal Wanderings through London

Dim lighting in the Polish café Daquise in South Kensington. An Asian man sits at the next table and grumbles quietly to himself about blacks and Jews in between slurps of his milky tea. The lime green earthenware cup looks like it's been well used: cracked and chipped like the varnish on the chairs. The waiter sighs as I pay. It has been a long day.

Drunks linger at the entrance to the Tube. Not one of them has the strength to even utter a swearword. A gust of wind sweeps the discarded section of the evening newspaper into their gaunt, expressionless faces. A seemingly unhinged woman asks me where she is and where she should go. She asks every passer-by this question. Youths urinate against the display windows of an upscale department store and brawl, swigging from beer cans and wine bottles that they subsequently smash against the kerb.

No, for once we will pass on the Tube. Even though it is night. Because it is night. Because London's nights entice. Even though there would be an exhibition still to see in Gloucester Road Tube Station: Guy Portelli's pictures, *Sea Life*. The colour worlds of the deep in the Underground world of the metropolis. Gloucester Road is the most culturally aware Underground station in London. Primarily turquoise, and the deeper you look, the bluer it seems: pure deep blue. The posters advertising this exhibition along the Piccadilly and District Lines show it. But I am in the mood for London's night, for the glimpse of sleeping parks and dark dinosaur-like houses, for paths that seem inevitably longer at night.

And so I reach Leicester Square after a while, on which the night air weighs heavily, enriched by a disagreeable sweetness, the smell of chips and beer. The stony face of the statue of Sir Joshua Reynolds, the great portraitist at the time of George III and first president of the Royal Academy of Arts, visibly lost its detail after officials decided to have it cleaned. Apparently, the specialists in cleaning stone monuments used such a harsh acidic cleanser that the identity of the face was erased. Perhaps the future of all monuments is that they will remind us of the neutralising of remembrance. As for the motto 'Learn to forget that you ever remembered': only forgetting still has a future. He who forgets best is likely to get ahead more easily.

Imagine it: Hogarth lived here at Leicester Square (Number 30); and Reynolds bought Number 47 in order to finally have premises in which he could open a gallery for his own paintings. This is where they went in and out, James Boswell, David Garrick, the greatest actor of the time, Fanny Burney and Edmund Burke. They had their portraits painted and admired, entertained and seduced, and were caricatured by Hogarth.

The Charlie Chaplin memorial seems to be more resistant to cleansers. You walk around him on plaques that show distances, as the crow flies. For example, it is a good 8,000 kilometres from here to Dhaka. It is a type of indicator for the almost 60,000 Bangladeshis who live in London.

I decide to move on. I move along a side street, passing an upmarket fish restaurant that is closing at this late hour. Cats slink around the dustbins that smell of fish. All cats look yellowish in London at night, due to the yellow light emanating from the street lamps. It is simply accepted that this light is yellow now. The gas lamps of yesteryear were not the same. They exuded a diffused white light that could not completely penetrate the darkness in London's streets. Edgar Allan Poe referred to this light when he described the amorphous London crowds as being as disjointed as the gaslight. Robert Louis Stevenson was also fascinated by the effects of gaslight and it defined his novel, *The Strange Case of Dr Jekyll and Mr Hyde* (1886). The evil Mr Hyde, into whom Dr Jekyll had transformed all himself thanks to the invention of a special drug, allied himself with the semi-darkness of gaslight. Evil flourishes in gaslight, which was twilight. Initially gaslight did not provide any real brightness at night; rather it crossed the darkness with traces of light, accompanied by the faint but constant hissing of the lamps.

Back to my blindingly illuminated London night. Chinatown would be a few steps from here. Beijing in London. But if you have read the Bi-Yaen-Lu in which is written what the Chinese of the 12th century held sacred, the 'open expanse', the heart, don't come to London's Chinatown.

Chinatown. I let myself drift through its alleys, following its aromas. Past the restaurant, Forbidden City, that advertises 'poetry in rice' with a poster. It smells of ginger and of nutmeg, as an older but seemingly agile man blocks my path. 'I, yellow man,' he said, and: 'I, flying bookseller.' And in no time, he spread a yellow silk cloth over a board he had laid across a rusting shopping trolley on which he then rapidly laid a couple of books. 'Yellow man recommend poems of Tang', and he grinned in my face and turned his head in such a manner that I had to look at him. '*The Silk Thread*, poem from Tang Dynasty, between 7th and 10th century,' he explained. 'Book, *Silk Threads*, bound in red silk with yellow ribbon. Souvenir of me, yellow man.' He hopped with joy, as though he achieved something special with this sentence. He wanted £2.50. A song for this attractively presented little volume. I bought it and gave him a £5 note. 'Rest for yellow man', he sneered at me and was already gone. Days later I read the line in *Silk Threads*: 'Cities will become retreats.'

I sauntered along Shaftesbury Avenue, the theatre street. It was in one of these theatres that I heard Edward Fox, that prototypical English actor with the seemingly bored and yet absolutely expressive stone face, and Ted Hughes as they read from the poems of T S Eliot, that English immigrant from St Louis, on the occasion of his 100th birthday in 1988. 'Unreal city ...' How often these lines repeat in one's thoughts when one exposes oneself to London? How often?

The performances have finished for today. People stream out of the theatres. Leaving them, as they entered them – as if they had seen nothing on the stage. I like to hang around the stage doors at this hour, where the actors and stage hands come out, the wardrobe mistresses and prompters, the lighting technicians and lavatory attendants. I wait at the stage door of the theatre in which Simon Callow has given his final performance in Peter Ackroyd's *The Mystery of Charles Dickens* (2000) this evening. I had seen the dress rehearsal for this one-man show at the Richmond Theatre, one of those repertory theatres in which plays are tried out and then, if successful, brought to London's West End.

Simon Callow *became* Charles Dickens in this part. What are *Starlight Express* or *Les Miserables* compared to this dramatic live monologue by an actor? Simon Callow as Dickens against the rest of the West End. Here he comes, Simon Callow, at best of middle height – like Dickens, a bit thickset – like Dickens, still gesticulating as he leaves the theatre. He still *is* Dickens. He may have left the theatre now, but not his part. It seems to me he has no choice but to go to Bloomsbury, to Number 48, Doughty Street, where Dickens completed *The Pickwick Papers*, wrote *Oliver Twist* (1837–9) and *Nicholas Nickleby* (1838–9). Callow increases his pace, gesticulates even more and actually moves in a northerly direction such that there can be no doubt that he is storming toward Doughty Street, as Dickens hurried through London. In fact it is amazing how much of London's atmosphere Dickens was able to bring into his novels as he admitted he was never able to stand at a street corner in London and truly observe. Dickens always absorbed impressions quickly, unlike Heine in Cheapside. He matched his powers of observation to his amazing pace. He was rarely accompanied as no one could keep pace with him, just as Simon Callow after embodying Dickens for the past two hours can only be alone now. To approach Simon Callow now would be ... an offence.

Of course there is a literary model for my nocturnal wanderings. Every step in this city has its predecessor. Even the simple act of stopping somewhere in London is described precisely in the many hundreds of novels about London: denying movement in this hectic hustle and bustle creates a stumbling block.

Dickens describes nocturnal wanderings in *The Old Curiosity Shop*:

'Night is generally my time for walking ... I have fallen insensibly into this habit, both because it favours my infirmity and because it affords me greater opportunity of speculating on the characters and occupations of those who fill the streets. The glare and hurry of broad noon are not adapted to idle pursuits like mine; a glimpse of passing faces caught by the light of a street-lamp or a shop window is often better for my purpose ... I must add the truth, night is kinder in this respect than day, which too often destroys an air-built castle at the moment of its completion, without the least ceremony or remorse.'

And as I have just mentioned the words 'stumbling block', the motto of our life (not just in London) may well be: Pause and reflect. And for this there is also a literary model, created by Paul Verlaine in his 'Sonnet Boiteux', written in 1872/3, when he visited London with Arthur Rimbaud and described the city like Babylon, as 'the city of the Bible'. The city became his torment, a big stumbling stone in his life:

> *Londres fume et crie. Ô quelle ville de la Bible!*
> *Le gaz flambe et nage et les enseignes sont vermeilles.*
> *Et les maisons dans leur ratatinement terrible*
> *Épouvantent comme un sénat de petites vieilles.*
>
> *Tout l'affreux passé saute, piaule, miaule et glapit*
> *Dans le brouillard rose et jaune et sale des Sohos*
> *Avec des indeeds et des all rights et des haôs.'*

Verlaine described Soho as a unique invitation to dance ('Dansons la gigue'). And in the foggy damp of Paddington, he saw water, paler than a dead woman, no longer capable of reflection. There is a charcoal sketch by Verlaine's friend, F-A Cazals, which shows the poet on a London street; a policeman is recognisable in the background. He stands there woodenly, seemingly robbed of movement. Perhaps he will turn to the bobby in a moment and make a police report against persons unknown, or against

London; because London has robbed him, the *flâneur*, not of speech, but of the desire to wander; at least that is how it appears. Verlaine's face looks like those faces the narrator of *The Old Curiosity Shop* likes to describe: which the street lamp illuminates only momentarily. In his poem written in Paddington, Verlaine says, there is no hope of Aurora ever shining on them or these black and fog-yellowed houses in the smoke, because somehow the sun does not seem appropriate to London.

In the meantime, I am approaching Charing Cross Road, passing pillar-boxes that have been sealed up due to a postal strike; Charing Cross Road, the street of booksellers. At least it used to be. These days, shop rents of up to £125,000 per year are demanded, which means the smaller dealers and specialists shops cannot hope to make a profit. Foyles, Quinto, Zwemmer, Al-Hoda and Silver Moon – those were the landmarks of this street. Not to mention Marks & Co, 84 Charing Cross Road, which was immortalised in Helene Hanff's eponymous novel about a transatlantic romance that develops simply from an inquiry about a book. I had to see my Lady in Yellow again in Charing Cross Road, at any time of day or night. She could once have settled in here, perhaps in Litchfield Street, at Zwemmer's.

I cross Shaftesbury Avenue and wait at a bus stop on its eastern side. Somewhere someone is calling for help. A car alarm starts up; then the siren of an ambulance. No one knows any details; no one wants to know. A beautiful black woman, clearly past her prime, grins at me. 'The Club is around the corner, man. Come along, if you like. You can get as many shots as you like there.' I respond that I was waiting for the night bus here, where upon she bursts into a suppressed, silent laughter which has her bent over double as if she were choking. She is still laughing when I board the bus. As the bus pulls away, I suddenly notice a long yellow scarf tied around the lamppost near the bus stop, waving in the night breeze like a flag. Or does the scarf only appear yellow, the same yellow as the London cats caught in the street lights?

6

The Omega of Bloomsbury

To Covent Garden: I wanted to go to the old Vanity Fair, to the Drury Lane Theatre, on a trail that should have led to *The Beggar's Opera*, the opera of the little man by the brilliant and anti-Handel John Gay. This is where the young, impoverished Dickens came to marvel at pineapples as the most exotic of fruits; where Hogarth and Boswell drank their coffee; and where Thomas de Quincy wrote his *Confessions of an English Opium-Eater* (1822). Covent Garden, where the vibrations of the leading operatic voices of the world seem to rest on the air.

But I missed getting off at the right Tube station, had fallen off into a daydream a good 100 metres underground, immersed in Virginia Woolf's small volume, *The London Scene*. My edition is protected by a yellow wipeable cover. Like a curtain or oversized keyhole it reveals a perspective of London's silhouette captured in pale shades of grey with a white gap for St Paul's Cathedral. Five brief essays about London, written in early 1930 by the mistress of modern prose. What did she write about? *The London Docks*, the *Oxford Street Tide*, *Great Men's Houses*, *Abbeys and Cathedrals* and the *House of Commons*. Seven printed pages per essay. Each essay matches the rhythms of the metropolis in its own way. Like all of Virginia Woolf's essays: twinkling crystals with subtle points: ' ... it is vain to try to come to a conclusion in Oxford Street'. Or another example: 'To look over London from this hill Keats came and Coleridge and Shakespeare, perhaps. And here at this very moment the usual young man sits on an iron bench clasping in his arms the usual young woman.' Or: '... all houses have voices ...'. So I was reading and Covent Garden was already behind me when I looked up from the pages.

In London you can intend to visit somewhere for weeks, months, even years and never get around to it. I would also claim you should ideally wait for certain times of day and year to visit certain districts, parts of town, streets. So it should have been a June evening for Covent Garden. But it is now a day in October, in the afternoon. The sky was part grey, part bright as I left the Tube station, in-between weather conditions that are now more typical for London than steady rain or fog. Umbrellas have disappeared for the most part from the street scene. London, it often seems to me, is moving in the direction of meteorological ambiguity.

So, no Covent Garden; rather, and why not, Bloomsbury. Today is still recognisably autumn, autumnal enough for Bloomsbury. Because it should be autumn in this area, around Russell Square; the leaves should be falling in front of the British Museum. The sallow yellow of the lights should have its effect, enveloping the passer-by and buildings rather than illuminating the streets.

At Russell Square Station there is an entrance at street level, as anywhere else, with ticket barriers. The barrier opens when you insert a valid ticket in the slot. These costly machines are like the counting machines cattle are run through in large abattoirs. But the ticket barriers are not working properly today at Russell Square. Instead, station staff are checking the passengers' tickets. Lost in thought, I show my yellow-grey book by Virginia Woolf instead of my ticket. It is only when the inspector waves me through that I realise my carelessness; but then I find the scene humorously appropriate and leave my ticket in my coat pocket. And thus she literally gave me entry to her Bloomsbury, Virginia Woolf with her *London Scene*. Now I know that this is how a London book should look: a mere 50 pages long, without a single illustration, the pages of heavy yellowish paper that one would ordinarily use for letters. To Bloomsbury then.

Wine grew here in the 11th century, and the woodland provided for at least 100 pigs, the ideal place to snuffle for truffles, so says the *Domesday*

Book, that infallible royal land register (quoted to this date with the same authority as the Bible) that William the Conqueror commissioned in 1086. Bloomsbury was originally named Blemondisberi, because this is where a certain William Blemond had his 'bury' or country seat. King Edward III granted this holding to the Carthusians and Blemondisberi became a monastery, with, it is said, an exemplary sewerage system. After the dissolution of the monasteries by Henry VIII, the Earl of Southampton was able to acquire the estate. After the Civil War, his son had the medieval walls torn down and in its place built Southampton House, with houses for the servants nearby and a fenced-in garden in the middle; this architectural design, which contemporaries greatly admired as one of the many 'English wonders', was named a square by the Earl (Bloomsbury Square today). John Evelyn, the second most important diarist and intellectual of his day after Samuel Pepys, came and admired it. He described the Square as 'a noble square or piazza – a little towne'.

The legendarily wealthy families of the Bedfords, Russells and Montagus followed suit and built their estates with 'piazzas' near Southampton (today Bloomsbury) Square; incidentally, Montagu House became the British Museum in the middle of the 18th century. Its present façade dates to the 19th century and was designed by Robert Smirke in Greek Revival style, and his younger brother Sydney designed the famous Reading Room with its copper dome and thus created the centrepiece of intellectual Bloomsbury.

Bloomsbury's legendary status, that Soho of intellectuals, is due less to the British Library Reading Room in which Thomas Carlyle, Karl Marx, Lenin and George Bernard Shaw worked, but rather to the authors, artists and academics who were young in 1910, usually from solid Victorian homes and rebelling against their parents' narrow-minded morality. Amongst them were Virginia Stephen and her sister Vanessa, the two daughters of the great Victoria scholar Leslie Stephen, Lytton Strachey, avowed homosexual and starving essayist, Roger Fry who introduced French Post-Impressionism to England, but derided German artists such as Dürer, the artists Clive Bell and Duncan Grant as well as the great macro-economist John Maynard Keynes who valued freedom within relationships more than anything else, and later also Leonard Woolf, a colonial civil servant highly critical of British imperialism.

Living in Bloomsbury was an act of faith as it was considered a bit run-down in comparison to high Victorian upscale Kensington, where Virginia and Vanessa had grown up at Hyde Park Gate. According to the soon-to-be-deemed 'disreputable' young intellectuals, Bloomsbury was supposed to be a small Montmartre, a Quartier Latin *à l'anglaise*. Except it lacked the bistros, the strolling areas, the flair. But they affected the avant garde, encouraged scandal, and considered themselves superior to everything and everyone. The centre point was formed by 46 Gordon Square where the Stephen daughters lived with their two brothers. After Vanessa's marriage to Clive Bell, who initially remained loyal to Gordon Square, Virginia and her brother Adrian moved to Fitzroy Square.

It would be misleading to imagine that Bloomsbury was the name for an internally homogenous group with a clearly defined sense of community. Nor was it an arena for unbridled passions. No, Bloomsbury represented a mostly Cambridge-educated individualism. Its hallmark was radical subjectivism as a collective experience. Thus whilst everyone spoke of free love, in reality most Bloomsberites were more faithful to their partners than many supposed Victorian paragons of virtue were to theirs. But the fact that literally everything was spoken about, every form of experience was reflected on, marked this group as different.

And yet, when it came down to really having to show openness in a very existential question, the Bloomsbury Group fell silent. I refer to the case of Angelica Bell, Vanessa Bell's daughter and thus Virginia Woolf's niece. It was late, too late for Angelica, when she discovered that Clive Bell was not her biological father, but the artist Duncan Grant, who normally was much more attracted to the male gender. Angelica Bell Garnett described her childhood and late trauma in a book she titled *Deceived with Kindness* (1984). She saw herself as the 'product' of an experiment that her love-starved mother had attempted with her bisexual friend.

Yes, Bloomsbury was the place of scurrilous contrasts, between sensitive thought and emphatically crude painting, between emphasis on sensitivity and the canonisation of reason-based 'healthy common sense', and between exotic esoteric individualism as embodied by the patron of the group, Lady Ottoline Morrell, and social public-spiritedness as espoused by Leonard Woolf. One claimed to be capable of the most precise reflection in any situation and yearned for a 'naïve' access to art. One lived in an ivory tower in a well-tended Square and conversed in the most cultured English, but paid homage to the philosophy of George Edward Moore, who was to publish his *A Defence of Common Sense* in 1925, but who had years earlier praised 'simple concepts', the value of everyday language and the naïve as the ultimate wisdom. For discussion during the scandal-ridden Thursday evening meetings of the Bloomsbury group was not just the question of what psychological effect a publicly committed sex act might have on the observers and the actors, but also the question of the opportunity to achieve new forms in art. The most important Bloomsbury theoretician in matters aesthetic, Clive Bell, produced a polemic against contemporary British art appreciation in 1914 laconically entitled *Art*; it was considered the most provocative writing on matters of art in English until 1930. Bell attempted to discover the 'significant form' in the artistic work of an artist; this significant form stimulates, according to Bell, our aesthetic experience: if it is working productively, it will react accordingly.

Roger Fry chose a more complex approach in his art theory. He based it not only on a careful study of *Notes d'un peintre* (1908) by Matisse, but also on the question of whether art was capable of making a contribution to the democratisation of society. The outcome of these deliberations was incorporated into his treatise *Vision and Design* published in 1920. This essay not only influenced the young Henry Moore, but also an entire generation of young artists in Great Britain who wanted to separate themselves from the superiority of western art traditions. In Bloomsbury Fry had pronounced the thesis that the 'naïve' use of art materials would make people more agreeable and human, decades before the German artist Joseph Beuys proclaimed the very same. If creativity in people was to be set free, it would not lead to fruitless lone wolves or mavericks, but rather to a social exchange – naturally, only when the pressure of competition is taken off artists. Fry claimed the artist should not strive for the highest, but rather what was to him closest, most immediately achievable. (Shaw scoffed later that Fry could only dream of what was closest because he was nearsighted.)

Nevertheless, the political tint that Fry brought to his perspective on art fits with our image of Bloomsbury: aestheticism and political-social engagement were no longer meant to put each other in checkmate. Aside from Leonard Woolf, no one embodied this reciprocal pollination of the artistic and political sense better than John Maynard Keynes. Keynes, in the manner of Chancellor of the Exchequer of the intellectual aristocracy of Bloomsbury, was more than a calculating economist and icy reckoner. He loved the 'economic experiment', which plainer souls would call a 'game'. As a 'practicing capitalist and erotomaniac', as he called himself, he experimented in the stock market, claimed to love stocks, mis-speculated, won at the 'race of the exchange', as he called it, and, in the end, became the only truly wealthy representative of Bloomsbury.

Like so many other Bloomsberites, Keynes was a pacifist during the First World War. Occasionally he was even suspected of being a German spy. His affection for Germany, however, was not made manifest until after the war. In his essay, *The Economic Consequences of the Peace* (1919), Keynes attacked the Allies' excessive reparations policy, because he assumed that this economic pressure would lead to instability and radical-isation in Germany and thus to new instability in Europe. Keynes' preoc-cupation with the German question represented an exception within the Bloomsbury group. To them 'overseas' meant France and Russia, with the beginnings of Soviet Communism. Consequently, discussions revolved around Matisse and Dostoevsky, Gauguin and Lenin. What the 'Prus-sians' were up to, on the other hand, whether with or without the Kaiser, was of little interest to anyone except Keynes. And the lack of interest was mutual. Who in Germany around 1920 had heard of Bloomsbury? An English avant garde in art? That was a contradiction in terms from both the Anglophile and Anglophobic German perspective. England only represented civil progress through technology. England – the industrial age times ten; it was the land of textile industries, banks and ghost stories. No one was aware that Bloomsbury, contemporaneously with Futurism in Italy and Novism in Russia, had initiated a true art movement. Vanessa Bell, Roger Fry and Duncan Grant founded their 'Omega Workshop' in 1913. They wanted to embody the omega of art, that final colourful, joyful, naïve condition of painting.

However, Omega also stood for escape from urbanism and social criticism. In the name of Omega, they moved to Charleston near Firle in Sussex. Surrounded by cow barns and duck ponds, they hoped for 'natural inspiration' from the obvious. What was the South Pacific for one and Arles for another, the county of Sussex was for the Bloomsbury artists. Everyone decorated their room individually at Charleston, painting what ever came within their reach – every chair, every cupboard, every inch of the originally lime-washed walls. Abstracts, however, were not allowed. Vanessa believed that nature was sufficiently rich that it should not be distorted through abstraction.

Keynes also came to review his economic theories with the farmers. Bloomsbury in the country. Omega as the connection between city and country, full of colour and a wealth of forms. Omega or the Triumph of Design Over Content. The 'ultimate' which was to be expressed by Omega's art drew its quality from the expression of the sub-conscious in colour. Vanessa, incessantly painting at Charleston, was as committed as her sister Virginia would be at the neighbouring Monk's House, continuously worrying about her writing. Freud had been read, but bizarre conclusions drawn – for instance that one should have to stylise one's artistic ego.

But Omega had another, more materialistic side as this art moved useful objects into the foreground, even though Rebecca West would sneer that Vanessa Bell's colourfully decorated plates were not worth putting your dog's raw mince on. Omega's colourful world of things makes the observer more or less conscious of his own thing-fetish; it parodies the supremacy of material things over man. Because things spew forth from us, Clive

Bell argued, like little red devils from the mouths of people in medieval paintings. When Bloomsbury had become its own fossil, Leonard Woolf claimed in 1947, six years after his wife's suicide, that it depended on how one cut this Bloomsbury rock. It could still be made into a gemstone, its value continually increasing. He could not possibly foresee that Laura Ashley would make a fortune from Omega designs in our time.

Oh, Bloomsbury. This is where University College stands, the wax effigy of its founder Jeremy Bentham mutely greeting the student body in College Hall, to this day dressed in authentic clothing including his favourite straw hat. The likeness is carried in a procession by men in livery to the first convocation of the College Senate. Bloomsbury – you can see it from afar, a landmark, a gigantic structure based on Stalinist architectural style, a greyish-white dinosaur of unusual ugliness, the Senate building of the University of London, once the Information Ministry during the war and for George Orwell the place that inspired his novel, *1984*. Bloomsbury – that is Russell Square, circumscribed by traffic and yet an oasis. Thackeray visited here regularly. And parts of the novel *Vanity Fair* took place here. Bloomsbury – welcome to the funfair of intellectual conceits. The young, slightly green T S Eliot made his first social appearance at Ottoline Morrell's parties. As a successful poet and advocate of a conservative modernity he then moved into an office in Russell Square, as editor and partner of the publisher George Faber.

There are traffic-becalmed Squares: Virginia's Fitzroy Square is one of them, presumably because the London Foot Hospital is located there. Leicester Square, despite its ceaseless floods of people, is also without traffic. If you have ever been sufficiently lucky to experience a square entirely devoid of people and traffic, you begin to have an inkling into the secret of these places. I had that good fortune one December morning in 1981 in Bedford Square; for London, which had no snowploughs, was numbed by masses of snow, paralysed, and overwhelmed. And Bedford Square belonged to itself and the pale yellow light that the street lamps shed, even during the day. You could hear nothing except the slight groaning of the snow-laden trees in the middle of the Square. The seemingly black houses with their white window surrounds set a stark contrast to this backdrop. Not a single pigeon cooed. The square maintained its silence about the city. Its houses seemed built of shadows. I went to its red pillar-box to post an imaginary letter. At the time, I thought I heard a very, very hollow laugh emanating from one of these houses.

Diversion IV

In the London of Emigrants

A fter having lived in London for some 25 years, one question had become pressing: why and for how much longer should one expose oneself to this urban mania with its absurd colourfulness and deafening multiplicity? A Swiss writer, who had been living in the rural retreat of the north of Ireland and who stopped off in London for a few days on his way from Glasgow to Zurich, asked me almost indignantly about the demands of this metropolis and its decaying infrastructure: How can you stand it? What he really meant was: How can you live with your conscience, spending your life in this juggernaut?

The more urgent the questions, the more hesitant the answers. Go back, I thought, go back to my student days on the mid-reaches of the Neckar, where I found myself listening to more and more music with British connections. Repeatedly Mendelssohn-Bartholdy's *Hebrides Overture*, frequently Thomas Tallis, Vaughan Williams, and then again Mendelssohn's *Scottish Symphony*, and Hans Werner Henze's opera based on Ingeborg Bachmann's *Der Junge Lord*. At some point, it seemed to me that I should have to follow these sounds to their country of origin. I attended lectures on English history (particularly about the Tudors) and read nothing but Virginia Woolf for weeks.

But there was another type of reading material. *Der verwaltete Mensch* ('The Administered Man', 1974) almost a thousand pages long, a sociological study of the heteronymous individual wrung from concentration camp experiences and *Das Antlitz einer Zwangsgemeinschaft* ('The Face of an Enforced Community', 1955), the subtitle of a study on Theresienstadt. Their author was H G Adler. Reading the minimal biography on the book jacket, I learnt only that he was born in Prague in 1910, survived Theresienstadt and Auschwitz, returned to Prague again and stayed there between 1945 and 1947, and then emigrated to London where he had lived as a scholar and writer ever since. In a journal I soon found poems by him and a short piece about his friend, the lyricist and anthropologist Franz Baermann Steiner, also from Prague, who spent his exile in London and Oxford, where he died in 1952. Steiner's verses sounded like a combination of Hölderlin and Eliot that had passed through Kafka and then were enriched by the knowledge of the anthropologist Steiner. In short, it struck a chord in me as I sat in my chair in the University of Tübingen library on the banks of the Neckar. A departure for England, for London and to Adler became inevitable.

An American student friend from Illinois countered these plans with the enticements of Santa Barbara, Yale or Evanston on Lake Michigan. In my ignorance, I claimed England was mid-way between them. And a few weeks later I drove, my Beetle packed to the roof, toward England, by way of Metz, Reims and along the Route Nationale 1 to Calais (the autoroute did not exist in those days), along the battlefields of yore or straight across them. Was I attempting to simulate the experience of exile?

I got as far as Calais and stayed the night in the Hôtel Windsor. The name seemed as appropriate as the view from the harbour across the Channel to the sparkling lights on the other side. I boarded the earliest possible ferry and for the first time saw the chalk cliffs of Dover: bare but luminescent, unapproachable yet alluring. There is something mysterious and risky about them. But I was not terribly interested in Dover. I was not familiar with it then, or Matthew Arnold's poem, *Dover Beach* (1867). Otherwise I might have said then 'neither love, nor joy, nor light, nor certitude, nor peace, nor help for pain' and would have probably turned about and returned on the next ferry, found refuge in Bruges or in Ghent or would have pushed ahead as far as Amsterdam the same day.

But I carried on to London, driving on the left for the first time, straight to Canterbury, my first stop on English soil. A poster advertised a performance of *Murder in the Cathedral* by T S Eliot. I purchased the text at a kiosk at the cathedral. As I entered, the slim volume slipped from my hand and fell on the threshold. A gust of wind or draught blew through the pages. I quickly bent to grasp the book and read: 'Wash the stone, wash the bone, wash the brain, wash the soul, wash them wash them!' I did not see much of the cathedral's interior at the time. They were busy with building a stage inside; several windows and columns were draped in black cloth. Lighting technicians were hard at work everywhere you looked and the cables were like mantraps.

I continued on towards London. Another 63 miles. First stop in Elm Park, in Essex. And it was here, the penultimate easternmost stop on the District Line, that I rang the Adlers, arranged a visit and finally made my way to Earl's Court, where H G Adler lived, on a grey October evening. 47 Wetherby Mansions.

Not yet equipped with that indispensable London map, the most important book of all about London, the *AZ*, with all conceivable streets and alleys; as yet unaware of the necessity of not taking a step without this London Bible if you are aiming for a specific destination in this city, I took a taxi from Earl's Court Station. As Wetherby Mansions lies only a few steps from Earl's Court Station, a fact I was ignorant of, the cab driver seized the opportunity and drove this clueless visitor around all the possible streets in the area, past hotels renting rooms by the hour and transient hotels for Asian asylum seekers, until the meter reached a point meaningful to him and we finally arrived, as if by a miracle, at Wetherby Mansions.

I stood in front of an imposing late Victorian mansion block with impressive doors and a large array of bells which showed no names, only numbers. In the yellow light of the street lamps, dampened by cold wisps of fog, I spotted an elderly, strikingly erect but very slow-moving gentleman, who was visibly suffering from asthma. I soon discovered that this was H G Adler. He had become worried when I did not arrive at the appointed time; and so he had wanted to go to Earl's Court Station, but then had to turn back due to the inordinate damp of the evening. Over-come with embarrassment, I mumbled a few words as a woman of inde-terminate age opened the door crying 'Where have you been?' and with nimble steps hurried down the stairs, carrying a mantle which she draped around her husband's shoulders.

The Adlers' flat was like a library, a museum, a memorial, a refuge, an artist's studio, a piece of transplanted Prague with its German-speaking Jewish middle class of yore. Whether he said it on the first or one of the following visits, I am not sure, but Adler emphasised that he treasured London, because one could disappear in it. Become anonymous. Dis-appear in the immense totality of it. I later read in his posthumously-published novel, *Die unsichtbare Wand* ('The Invisible Wall', 1989), the sentences about London by Adler's *alter ego*, Artur Landau, who leaves some hope in the end: 'Let me disappear in the cosmopolitan city. It is incalculable, confused, eerie; I have yet to understand why. But it has mysterious neutrality, completely different from the big cities I know over there. You cannot belong to this city, yet you are in it, independent, almost free, you are little touched by it and everyone minds their own business. I can foresee that I will never be completely lost specifically because of its forlornness.'

Like so many émigrés, Adler both treasured this anonymity and suf-fered from it. He spoke in this silvery Prague German, told of Max Brod, referring to a verse by the German poet Klopstock and with a single reach of his arm grabbed a first edition of his songs. We spoke of Elias Canetti, of Arnold Schönberg's compositions and those by E T A Hoffmann, which he valued more than any other, but only seldom, very seldom, of anything or anyone English.

His most intense contacts seemed to be with young people in Germany, who turned to him when they encountered difficulties with the Nazi past of their parents. And he gave advice, showed an interest in the problems of the young generation, as though he too belonged to it. He demonised no one, condemned no one, but rather attempted to understand. He made no accusations; rather he enlightened. His sociology resembled an anatomy of suffering. After this first meeting (dozens more would follow in the years to come), I could hardly avoid coming to perceive London from the perspective of an exile myself.

The diaries of the most European of Austria's great writers of the past, Stefan Zweig, were published at this time. Parts written in England, London in particular, quite accurately characterised the shadow world of exile and foreignness, the constant struggle for acceptance. In September 1935 he travelled from Paris to the Thames and crossed 'England's green and pleasant land' in the southeast by train:

'And then finally London, after these unspeakably ugly, grey and rusted suburbs, tantalised by the occasional gracious glance of green, followed by the explosion of words in full and varied illumination from the rooftops and shops in all colours, yellow and green and red and blue, sparkling cries of light amidst the sinking sun, names, goods and words intended to animate purchase, on every level they jump out at you in the streets: buy! buy! buy! A horribly monotonous imperative. But wonderfully constant the endless stream of motorcars between the traffic lights. This is where the world shows its other face, the sensible one, the technical one; here in the practical world, our European present, which is failing so totally in the spiritual, shows its wastefulness in its arts and crafts. One senses the enormity of this city once again, stretching out over five continents like a polyp with a thousand tentacles, to suck its power, its riches, its energy into itself, which transforms the invisible work of invisible millions into light and luxury and wealth and movement thanks to the dangerous miracle of our world, the organisation. [...] Down to Piccadilly Circus then, this round plaza, the actual North Pole or South Pole of our world, around which the planet rotates. It is difficult to remain standing still there, so strong does the movement vibrate; one is pushed and shoved by the swarm, one is blinded by the pushing of the motor cars, one is deafened by the roaring; and yet, one remains specifically to savour this dynamic force.'

Stefan Zweig is standing in Piccadilly Circus as Heine once did in Cheapside. He wants to be overwhelmed by impressions, yet still wishes to see himself reaffirmed in his ambivalence. Yet despite all doubts with respect to this maelstrom, this is a person who somehow tries to make a new home here, despite the insanity of this city: 'The longer I stand here, the more I can feel this whirling force. It has turned evening. Now all the motor cars and buses and underground trains of this city of six million are storming toward this little area in Soho that incorporates nine-tenths of all theatres and show booths and pleasures of London. With one lurch, at half past eight they will all begin, for an hour, at 11 all will end. Simultaneously, the actors are singing and dancing and playing, figures are running across the cinema screen, a human army, three army corps or six or ten, I do not know, collectively exercising their emotion. And amongst them one is alone, thrilled and reluctant, falling under the spell of this concurrence and yet cursing it, captured by the polyp arm of this big city and resisting against it; but without one being aware of it, after one hour or two, one grows accustomed to its rhythm. And it accompanies one all the way to one's sleep. The next morning, I know it, I am no longer a stranger here and can return to my work, pulled together and refreshed, can attempt to make sense of this duality with my small strength.'

A tragic illusion, as it soon turns out for Zweig. Exile would wear him down: in London and Bath and finally in Brazil. I admit I try to imagine Stefan Zweig in London from time to time. Zweig in Portland Place, then around the corner in Hallam Street with Regent's Park just a few steps away; Zweig in the British Library where he keeps searching for material for libretti that he could pass on to librettists the Nazis approved of, so Richard Strauss would finally have something to compose again in Garmisch; Zweig, how he repeatedly tries to tear himself away from London, travelling to Portugal with his secretary, lover and later second wife, Lotte Altmann; how he explores New York, as well as 30 other cities in the United States during his American lecture tours, in addition to Paraguay, Argentina and Brazil, as though they might be suitable as new places of exile. All because London cold-shouldered him for the most part, although his English publisher endeavoured to look after him, and he had friends on the Thames ... more than he was willing to admit. But no real public acclaim. Only once, on 26 November 1939, in the crematorium at Golders Green in the north of the city, when he delivered a eulogy over Sigmund Freud's coffin, and for just a brief moment it was like it had been in Vienna ... Yes, every now and again, I try to imagine what it must have been like for Stefan Zweig, standing in Piccadilly Circus, in the shadow of Eros in aluminium, the red light district of Soho within reach: 'And amongst them one is alone.' Even when accompanied by friends, even when he was with Lotte.

They have become ever more present for me, the emigrants of days gone by, even those who lived here around 1850, banned from the German states. Arnold Ruge, the upright democrat and doyen of German exiles around that time; Gottfried Kinkel, the theologian turned agnostic, as well as art and literary historian, for a few weeks a type of Garibaldi during the Baden Revolution of 1849, and his wife Johanna, a writer by trade (her posthumously-published autobiographical novel *Hans Ibeles in London* (1860) offers a fairly graphic account of the living conditions of exiles at the time); and the 'Mother of Exiles', friend of Richard Wagner's, and champion of female emancipation, Malwida von Meysenbug; and of course Karl Marx. Meysenburg worked as governess in the home of Alexander Herzen in Euston Square, who wrote long letters to her about political philosophy, although they lived under the same roof.

Kinkel became a lecturer on German art and literature, their development and current condition around 1850, at London's University College and in Edinburgh where he gained a popularity that would border on a fairytale in today's world. Marx, who felt himself isolated, envied this 'pretty boy' his success with the 'aestheticising Jewish bourgeoisie'(!) and described, not without malice, Kinkel's performance. He apparently never looked up from his script and his rather confused thoughts were cloaked in miserable English. Marx suggested the tumultuous applause that Kinkel invariably reaped was an expression of relief that the lecture was at an end.

A major contribution to Kinkel's popularity was an article published in 1850 in *Household Words*, the influential journal edited by Charles Dickens. It was written by Richard Horne, already encountered briefly as writer of *Memoirs of a London Doll*. Horne portrayed Kinkel as a martyr for freedom, who was imprisoned in Prussia for his liberal views and put to work at a spinning wheel where he had to spin thread for 13 hours a day.

And then there is Ferdinand Freiligrath, a German writer who was exiled for his democratic beliefs in 1848 and suffered from anonymity in London and yet became one of the most important translators of Coleridge into German, and who wrote of his sojourn in the so-called Hackney Downs in north London:

'An der Weltstadt nördlichem Saum,
Fern von ihrem Gebrause,
Bei der Pappel, dem Ulmenbaum,
Ländlich steht meine Klause.'

In this poem, Freiligrath speaks of being on the northern edge of the city, far from all the noise, finding his rural retreat under the trees, the poplars and the elms. He was searching for a hermit as his ideal and found himself.

Since my encounters with Adler, my entire sympathies belong to exiles, those once uprooted, living out of suitcases, whose enforced mobility at the time now appears like a tragic beacon for our lives in a global world. Those exiles with their accent-heavy tongues, whose English seems like a linguistic mirror of their own deformed identities, often possessing nothing more than their will to survive. They were subjected to humiliation and bureaucratic absurdities in their host country (which, incidentally, drove Stefan Zweig mad about England). They alternated between efforts at assimilation bordering on self-denial (usually associated with changes of name) and an enhanced self-confidence; and these ambivalences live on in their children.

Curious how exile nourished the patriotic feelings of some emigrants for the country of their torment. After Malwida von Meysenburg had watched the Duke of Wellington's funeral procession in November 1852, she noted in a letter: 'I was particularly delighted that the spiritual and aesthetic elements of these celebrations were German.' She was alluding to Beethoven's funeral march being played and that the grandiose hearse had been designed by the architect Gottfried Semper, who himself had become an exile in London after his participation on the Dresden barricades.

Exiles – they either remain amongst themselves or assimilate as quickly as possible, attempting to become more English than an English Londoner could ever be. Exiles, the tragedians of the modern age, driven away by the totalitarian demand of certain ideologies, survivors, shipwrecked, forced into an existence in the in-between; because they never quite arrive in their new country, they have their native country in their luggage and their accent.

When the Austrian poet Theodor Kramer, with the help of Franz Werfel, Thomas Mann and Arnold Zweig, in addition to financial assistance of The English Centre of PEN, managed to leave Vienna at the last minute (it was July 1939) and emigrated to London, he found himself thrown into the life-saving foreignness and paid the price with profound loneliness. When his sole publication in exile appeared in 1943, the lyrical cycle, *Verbannt aus Österreich* ('Banned from Austria'), it also contained a poem which most poignantly reflects a displaced person's state of mind in the London metropolis.

In this poem he speaks of the crooked alleyways surrounding Leicester Square; how, despite the decay and dilapidation of the surrounding buildings, the desire for survival forcefully takes everyone over even during the day; of the prostitutes who know what it takes to energise the tired, exhaust the strong, all spiced with bitterness; how man continues to try to live his life in an orderly fashion no matter what is thrown in his way; and finally, how the stranger feels uniquely at home in these alleys, having once had his spirit broken in his homeland, this new land is doing it to him once again.

For the exile, whether in London or elsewhere, time stands still, and yet he believes he must hurry along. How can we remain calm, with him in mind?

7

Westminster – Poetry in the Shadow of Power

'Man does not end with the limits of his body or the area comprising his immediate activity. Rather, the range of the person is constituted by the sum of effects emanating from him temporally and spatially. In the same way, a city consists of its total effects, which extend beyond its immediate confines. Only this range is the city's actual extent in which its existence is expressed.' The Berlin sociologist Georg Simmel's observation from 1903 (*Die Großstädte und das Geistesleben; Metropolis and Intellectual Life*) without a doubt also describes London to the extent that one accepts the metaphor of the body. In particular it could be said of the parish of Westminster Abbey, with St James's in the north, Victoria Station in the west and the Strand and Embankment in the east: the core of the many cores of London.

Westminster and the sum of its significance – which includes the mythologizing of Parliament in the form of Westminster Hall (built in 1097), which escaped the ravaging fire of 1834 that took all the other remaining buildings of the former Palace of Westminster as sacrifices. This is where the young Dickens came, after his very first article was published in *Monthly Magazine*, to think about his future. Victoria Tower rises above it, with its legendary parliamentary archive and parchment scrolls of royal and parliamentary decrees, a hoard of legal precedents that reaches back to the reign of Henry VII, a unique library of the literature of power.

Until the 18th century justice was dispensed in Westminster Hall and booksellers set up their stalls in it. It was here that Charles I was sentenced (1649) and Cromwell elevated himself to 'Lord Protector' (1653) or dictator in the name of Puritan Protestantism. After the Restoration, a macabre decoration was added to this venerable hall: Cromwell's skull crowned the roof for 25 years, until a storm swept it into the Thames.

And over there, the Abbey, where for several centuries the two archrivals of the British Isles, Elizabeth I and Mary Stuart, have lain virtually next to each other. At Poets' Corner the bards of the land lay buried, or are remembered with busts fashioned posthumously. One of them, in particular, is unforgettable if you allow it to work on you for more than a moment: Jacob Epstein's bust of William Blake, which was erected here in 1957 on the 200th anniversary of the poet's birth; Blake the dreamer with the piercing look; Blake, this stone guest of nightmares; Blake, who saw his London populated by mythical creatures; deemed a madman during his lifetime, that lunatic from Soho. Thomas Hardy's body was interred here, but not his heart, which was kept in a biscuit tin and then be interred amongst his ancestors in the churchyard of Stinsford in Dorset.

Name upon name: Coleridge, John Gay, Thomas Grey, Dickens and also learned men: Gilbert Murray, classicists like the Prussian orientalist John Ernest Grabe, who anglicised himself just as a certain George Friederic Handel did after him and Isaac Casaubon from Geneva, the scholar of scholars whose name was used by George Eliot in *Middlemarch* to characterise an arch scholar. No, she is not commemorated here in Poets' Corner; Mary Ann Evans from Nuneaton near Coventry created too much of a scandal for Victorian England when as George Eliot she lived in sin with Goethe's biographer George Henry Lewes, in Regent's Park.

Poets' Corner – it resembles a noble counterpart to Speakers' Corner in Hyde Park, except no one stands on a soapbox here, but rather with dignity on a marble column. Here, at Poets' Corner, you could picture the most select disputations between dead writers and scholars; the most noble silence imaginable is assured in this corner of Westminster Abbey. Tennyson, spoiled by success, versus the overly reflective Coleridge versus the greatest English orator of the 18th century, Richard Brinsley Sheridan. Or how about a debate between Henry Irving, the great Shakespearean actor, and John Gay, the creator of *The Beggar's Opera*? I would like to listen to James Macpherson, the translator (or inventor) of the Ossian cycle of poems and Dr Samuel Johnson, who rests within eyeshot and who branded Macpherson as a publicity-seeking fraud.

And then she appears between the busts and marble graves – my Lady in Yellow; she is wearing a black lace shawl, probably Florentine or Brussels lace, draped over her yellow dress, very attractive, I have to admit; she is even wearing black gloves; the only thing missing is a black head covering. She is leafing through a volume of Byron, without removing her gloves. She is apparently searching for the memorial plaque for the Lord of Poets. He died on 19 April 1824, 36 years old, in Missolonghi, Greece. A wreath of dried roses covers part of Byron's epitaph: 'torture and time' is legible and ' ... breathe when I expire'. Robert Browning lies nearby, having been transferred from Venice to Westminster Abbey, but his wife Elizabeth Barrett Browning was not; he had to bury her in Florence in 1861.

The Brownings, *the* couple of poetry. Someone should now play some Chopin, because I always associate Elizabeth Barrett Browning, the far more talented of the two, with Chopin, with pain, with southern melancholy, with a last languishing look out the window of Casa Guidi on to the hustle and bustle in the alleys below. Robert Browning, on the other hand, was the romantic turned into the ponderous. His heavily overplayed, poetry can be off-putting. But his wife wrote verses like this one: 'Thou comest! all is said without a word./ I sit beneath thy looks ...'. She is not interred here, rather she lies at the Arno with her Florentine hat, which she loved.

And now my Lady in Yellow with black ribbons, does she not strangely resemble Elizabeth Barrett Browning, the manner in which she stands there, the pale face framed by thick, curled dark brown hair, more hair than face? What was amongst the last things created by Elizabeth? A drawing. The drawing of a fig tree under which she sat in October 1860.

I have it with me, a framed photocopy of Elizabeth Barrett Browning's fig tree sketch. That is why I came here, to place it on Robert Browning's tombstone. And whilst my mourning clad Lady in Yellow continues to search for Byron's plaque, I approached Browning's somewhat pitiful-looking black stone. It was inevitable that we should run into one another, near the spot of John Milton's bust. But she turns away, towards the memorial plaque of Winston S Churchill, the Nobel Prize Winner for Literature (1953) from 10 Downing Street. It was his six-volume history, *The Second World War*, that earned him this honour, exaggerating his achievements in the field of literature because the said history is a compilation of average-calibre journalism. (Remember that Churchill won the Nobel Prize for Literature and James Joyce did not; this thought can leave one stunned for weeks.)

But to return to what is truly important: my Lady in Yellow with Florentine mourning lace cannot stop here either; rather she takes a forbidden seat in the choir stall and reads Byron by the glow of a Eucharist candle. Meanwhile, I deposit the framed, photocopied fig tree at the Browning stone and go outside.

I am standing there as though unable to do anything else. A sense of awe shivering down my spine, at a loss, deafened by the unending roar of background noise, enveloped by the long shadows. Remembering who has come this way before, carried to his grave or led to the altar; one would like to sink into the ground, flushed with shame. Joseph Addison, first publisher of *The Spectator*, that legendary journal which first defined a democratic self-awareness of British intellectuals, wrote around 1711 that he frequently visited Westminster Abbey because the sight of the graves and busts killed any stirrings of envy and awakened in him a hope to join these souls after death.

But there is another aspect to this. At this spot you stand in the turning circle of power, at the zenith of any London experience; in Westminster you find yourself less convinced than ever; no, more confused than ever would be more accurate. You think you are a republican, and yet you cannot deny feeling some momentary royalist sentiments and smile at this insular traditionalism. Constitutional patriotism as an antidote crosses my mind, and I swallow dryly. Big Ben rings out five times: the one and only true Westminster bell, different from those reproduced imitation sounds of countless mantelpiece clocks and others with comparable sound-effects.

Here in the district of power was the intended target of what would have been the biggest terrorist attack in the history of the British Isles. It was to have taken place in the now only vaguely remembered Palace of Westminster and was designed to destroy the entire royal family and members of Parliament in both houses – Commons and Lords. The terrorists belonged to a large group of Roman-Catholic Britons who felt oppressed by James I, the Protestant convert son of Mary Stuart. They wanted to win religious tolerance by this horrific act.

The attack was planned for 5 November 1605. Betrayal within the ranks of the conspirators frustrated it at the last moment. The royal guard captured Guy Fawkes in the act of making final preparations amidst the countless powder kegs and fuses in the cellars under the Palace. Under torture in the Tower he gave up the names of his fellow conspirators. Several of them were killed out of hand, others dragged through London to their executions. All of their heads were displayed on pikes in Parliament Square, subjected to general contempt. Since that day the cellars of the Houses of Parliament are symbolically searched before every State Opening of Parliament.

Writing under the sign of power. It is remarkable how many British politicians are writers – to this day. In addition to Disraeli and Churchill, the notorious former Chairman of the Conservative Party Jeffrey Archer, the former Foreign Secretary Douglas Hurd, the former Home Secretary Kenneth Baker, who attempted to make a name for himself as an anthologist of English poetry, and on the other side of the political divide, Barbara Castle and foremost of all Tony Benn, the Labour veteran of aristocratic birth and a truly significant diarist in the tradition of Pepys and Evelyn.

Attempting to understand the meaning of power by literary analysis appears to have drawn a number of the most important British writers repeatedly into the orbit of Westminster. None was more successful at this than the Victorian novelist Anthony Trollope, who also made a career in the Royal Mail. Trollope's novel, *The Prime Minister* (1876), offers a savage analysis of the politics of interest and influence as the principal factor in the game for power. Michael Dobbs also succeeded, during the Thatcher years, in presenting a breathtaking analysis of the unscrupulous machinations and intrigues in Westminster with his novel, *House of Cards* (1989). The television series of this, broadcast on BBC1, was a ratings triumph in the last days of Thatcher's premiership, accompanying and reflecting her downfall.

Ian McEwan also engaged in literary political analysis in his novel, *The Child in Time* (1987), in which beggars are required to be licensed and yet are forbidden to operate in Westminster, Whitehall and Parliament Square. A variety of authorities chase the beggars and homeless around the city, while claiming to be doing something for their physical fitness as a consequence (in my edition of *The Child in Time*, the printer's devil spoke the truth: in numerous places, it reads 'Westmonster' rather than 'Westminster'!). But even Ian McEwan did not go as far as William Morris, the great aesthete of the Labour movement and apostle of, as he referred to it, socially acceptable curlicue designs, who envisaged Parliament Square as an enormous fertiliser market in his utopian novel, *News from Nowhere* (1891).

Henry James once called the Houses of Parliament the best club in London; and Virginia Woolf spent a day in the Visitors' Gallery of the Commons to get a sense of how history is made. But she saw only politicians, who had already been frozen into their own statues and were simply waiting to be carried out to Parliament Square to be erected next to Gladstone, Pitt and Palmerston. She observed Stanley Baldwin and his opponent, Ramsay MacDonald, and asked herself what type of marble might be appropriate for them. And in no time, a little essay about Virginia's afternoon in the Lower House becomes a piece of literature.

I cross Old Palace Yard and go to the Victoria Tower Gardens on the banks of the Thames, where stands a copy of Rodin's stirring group sculpture, *The Burghers of Calais*: bent, emaciated but not broken, ready to sacrifice themselves for their city, to deliver themselves to their fate in the form of the English king. There they stand – in the shade, their eyes lowered so far that they cannot see the Thames and its sluggish, indifferent flow. I look across to the other bank with their eyes.

There, Lambeth Palace seems to rest on its laurels, the London palace of the Archbishops of Canterbury; and there, downstream, the millennium London Eye, that giant ferris wheel, turns. A little bit of Vienna's Prater and Disneyland in one, designed by David Marks and Julia Barfield, sponsored by British Airways. The high-tech pods were built in France, the ball bearings came from Germany, the framework manufactured of British steel in Holland, the cables came from Italy and the spokes are of Czech design. The 'Eye' is now for Londoners what the Eiffel Tower is for some and the Empire State Building is for others: the eye of eyes. It developed out of the need for a comprehensive view, to capture London as a panorama.

And that is the key word: panorama. The Irishman Robert Barker once erected a rotunda in Leicester Square, to display his panoramas. This was in 1793. The alternative revolution, not a storming of the Tower or Bastille, but a radical alteration of perspectives. To capture the world in the circular. Once around Barker's Panorama in Leicester Square saved a long walk through the filth of the city. The city experience in a time warp. And now Marks, Barfield & Co have simply turned Barker's 1793 Panorama by 90 degrees and even relieved the observer of the need to walk around the rotunda by turning the rotunda into a giant wheel (a diameter of 135 metres). The panorama pictures can also be dispensed with; after all you can see London life from these expensively constructed cabins, though you are spared the true living conditions by the grace of distance. This slow-moving (0.6 miles per hour) ride is officially called a 'flight', courtesy of the main sponsors, and as with an airline flight, you are given a boarding pass. You pay a considerable sum to become a captive of the 'must see'. Never has one been able to see more of London and, at the same time, less than in this forced viewing chamber. You can see for 40 kilometres on a clear day. Forty kilometres in all directions and nothing but London.

Diversion V

In London with Fontane

I wonder whether there is something dubious or incriminating about travelling with poets in your luggage. With Philip Roth around New York. With Dostoevsky around St Petersburg. With Nadine Gordimer around Cape Town and with Joseph Conrad into the heart of African darkness. Because it is part of a writer's art to direct his potential readers' view, to commit them to his perspective.

One perhaps even more problematical variation: to experience a city by means of the interpretation of a poetic cityscape, as interpreted by yet another author. One of many examples: Ernst Jünger on Dostoevsky's view of London. In his controversial book, *Approaches: Drugs and Ecstasy* (1970), Jünger adopted Dostoevsky's view and edits it to reflect his own view in the chapter, 'Books and Cities':

'In Paris, Dostoevsky found "calm in the orderliness – a colossal, internal, emotional, soul-based adherence to rules and regulations. Could be a gigantic Heidelberg." London appears to him as the titanic negative of this calm humanity contained within all this movement. A "fear of something" begins to claim him on walks through this city in which "half a million working men and women pour like an ocean into the streets with their children every Saturday evening, crowding into particular parts of town to celebrate the entire night until five in the morning; meaning they stuff themselves like animals and drink to excess after the entire week of starvation." These millions carry their entire week's wages in their pockets, everything they have earned with their hard labour. The gas burns in clumps of flames in the meat and grocery shops, illuminating the streets with their glare. It is almost as if a ball is being given in honour of these white Negroes. The pubs are decorated like palaces. Everyone is drunk, but without jollity; it seems more gloomy, heavy and peculiarly silent. Only every once in a while is this suspicious taciturnity interrupted by curses and bloody fights. The women are not outdone by the men and drink as much as they do; the children walk and crawl amongst them ...

[...] Apparently Dostoevsky found something calming behind the lack of monotony in Paris and something frightening in the orderliness of London.'

Jünger describes what he believes Dostoevsky saw in London: Hogarth's *Gin Lane*, the street of the damned, multiplied by a million, a century later. There are literary gems that do not fade. This quotation is one of them. One does not forget it, even if one might have somewhat different experiences of a Saturday in London. (By the way, the other day I saw a still life at the Tate Modern by a Flemish master as the subject of a computer simulation, in which the fruits rot in time-lapse before your eyes.)

What would it be like to be accompanied through London by Theodor Fontane? That would have appeal. Led by Brandenburgian sobriety through the mystery that is London. However, unlike Paris, London was often disenchanting to the eyes of the 19th century. When Victor Hugo wrote one of the first modern city novels (*Notre-Dame de Paris*) in 1831, he described the metropolis on the Seine as phantasmagoric and a 'fountain and sewer of civilisation'.

Fontane, on the other hand, always approaches the phenomenon of London with irony, for example in his notes on London from around 1850 and also in his last novel, *Der Stechlin* (1899). When young Woldemar von Stechlin prepares himself for a diplomatic mission to London, he seeks the advice of a family with experience of England, which recommends the following, relatively simple sightseeing itinerary: 'In Italy you waste your time with paintings, in England with execution blocks. They have entire collections of those over there. So keep the historical to a minimum.' On the other hand, they recommend that he experience the city as a land-scape with Richmond Hill and the quiet squares and a manifestation of art because of the many street artists who cover the pavements with their near masterpiece copies of Raphaels, da Vincis and the like.

But then comes the keyword, which not only provides a sudden insight to the point underlying the five chapters on England in *Der Stechlin*, but also to Fontane's thorough pre-occupation with British culture: England being that country to which everything returns, the country of repetition, in other words not of limitless, but rather repeatable opportunities and therefore London is the capital of tradition-bound repetition. Because there tradition defines the limitations of what is possible.

This thought also occurred to other writers travelling to England after Fontane. Wolfgang Koeppen, for example, wrote in his 1958 sketch of London (*Zauberwald der roten Autobusse*), that in England, and particu-larly in London, 'at any moment a stock market coup can be gained, an empire can be conquered and the Battle of Trafalgar can be fought and won'.

So what did Fontane's Woldemar von Stechlin actually absorb about London? Did he 'learn to see', like Rilke's Malte in Paris? Only very little. The reader does not experience him in a real London. The locale for his England adventures remains the anglicised Berlin salon of the Barby family. 'I saw nothing in particular which astounded or even enraptured me', he admits. The Pre-Raphaelites impressed him to some degree, as did the seascapes by Turner and the sarcophagi of the two queens at enmity, Elizabeth and Mary Stuart. What moved him was the feeling that 'between these two opposites world history' oscillated, specifically the 'opposites of passion and calculation, of beauty and wisdom', of merits and demerits through which the historical development in the sense of constant return of opposites is maintained.

Fontane spent two weeks in London in 1844 and half a year in 1852, and then from 1855 to 1859 as press correspondent of the Prussian embassy, Fontane noted before his first journey to the island that he looked to England as the Jews in Egypt looked to Canaan. And truly no country seemed to him more laudable, no foreign culture more agreeable, but also worthy of criticism. In his diary he initially rhapsodised the glow of the sinking sun over the domes of the city like his fellow writers normally raved about the roofs of Rome and Florence. In some domes of London he even saw future minarets in the city of the Prophet. But of which prophet and for which prophecies?

London, for an enthusiastic 'Anglomaniac', as he referred to himself at times, was the 'boldly arched bridges' and the 'fairy tale-like splendour of the illuminated West End'. In London he sees 'the model or quintessence of an entire world'. But – model of which world? These were the questions of his studies and travel features on England and Scotland, the journal notes and letters that he authored during his time in Victorian Great Britain. The 'Prophet' in London? Was that the stockbroker or still Shakespeare, whose presence he experienced through the stirring performances of Edmund Kean on the London stage and which he compared to the antiquated productions of Shakespeare on the Berlin stage? What was announcing itself in this teeming metropolis?

The fact that Fontane's analysis of British culture was soon accompanied by disillusionment with the realities of everyday life (particularly in London) did not prevent him from continuing to be capable of subtle observations of this culture.

Amongst the earliest, and most enduring, impressions Fontane gained of London was a sociological and architectural one: 'The magic of London is – its massiveness', he wrote, and: 'The bridges are, in my opinion, by far the most significant that London has to show with respect to buildings.' The power of the masses and the disappearance of the ego were Fontane's primary observations in London. He spoke of 'lavish affluence', of the 'inexhaustible mass' of this metropolis and explained: 'When one is looking down on this sea of houses from St Paul's or the Greenwich Observatory – whether one wanders through the City streets and, half dragged along by the human tide, one cannot suppress the thought that every building must be a theatre, that is just now releasing its audience swarms into freedom – everywhere it is the number, the multitude, that compels our amazement.'

This is where one wants to maintain perspective; and for this purpose he seeks an exposed place and is only able to acknowledge a sense of being overwhelmed. His 'I' was left no choice in the face of this enormity but to become an anonymous 'one'. The blaze of the setting sun, 'seas of fire' over the city as Fontane termed it, contribute something threateningly enchanting to the scenario of the masses. The smithy of the Industrial Age is projected like a beacon onto the evening sky over London: the beginning of a new age and at the same time, the signal of its demise.

However, Fontane saw not only the threatening massiveness of London, but also the connection between the masses and the massiveness of bridges to which he specifically attributed 'individuality'. He was particularly keen on Southwark Bridge with its 'granite parapet' and the three 'giant bows', each with a span of 240 feet, as he precisely noted. Bridges appeared to Fontane to be significant signs of the dissemination and development of civilisation. But when he composed a ballad on the collapse of the bridge on the Tay, he recognised this catastrophe as a symbol of civilisation's fragility.

In any event, Fontane depicted Victorian Great Britain, and, in particular, London, as the place of the over-sized, even of the gigantic. When he visited the Crystal Palace, built by John Paxton to house the Great Exhibition, but which had since been abandoned, he saw in its colossal size something almost morbid, grotesque even; he referred to this 'glass body' as a 'giant corpse' and attached to it the following reflection, which impressively complements his considerations on the 'massiveness' of the British metropolis:

'There is something peculiar about the absolute power of the space! The ocean and the desert – they have this charm, and quietly I felt myself touched by it, as my eye measured the enormous dimensions of this palace. The impression may have been lovelier, more pleasing when an entire world had spread its best out here; but it was no less impressive. And, as I moved through this space, from column to column and, almost exhausted by the total uniformity and constant repetition of all individual parts, yet not able to stop admiring the gigantic totality, it appeared to me that this glass house was as an image of London itself: revolting monotony in detail but fullest harmony in totality.'

For Fontane, London proves itself to be the backdrop for modern civilisation, which is not permanently fixed, but rather based on permanent change (which does not exclude repetition!) by discarding the decrepit and exhausted. Little time remains for reminiscing:

'Our time moves along rapidly: they are as quick to create as they are to destroy; one more winter and the Glass House will be in ruins. Already wind and dust are penetrating hundreds of broken panes, already the red cloth of the benches is torn and faded, and already the spider has made this her home and has woven her grey veil, the old flags of destruction. So be it. The trees, which Paxton's bold hand incorporated into his glass structure, are greening again, and speak of rejuvenation; and while the wind and sand may blow in through the gaps in the windows, even the swallows flutter in and speak to each other of life and undying love amongst the ruins.'

The break-in of nature into civilisation: for Fontane the trail of decline leads to the most poetic comparisons in the area of greater flourishing flora and fauna. Fewer metaphors and we believe we can hear the old Stechlin, who will say: 'The "I" is nothing – that is something one has to come to terms with. An eternal truth is at work, nothing more, and this implementation, even if it is called "death" must not frighten us. Putting oneself within the lawfulness is what makes the moral man and raises him.' Of course it requires a well developed 'I' to derive such insights and stand by them.

A further question troubles Fontane in London: how does the scale of this hugeness, this enormity, compare, if at all, to its practical function and symbolic meaning? He attempted to address this in the context of the new Parliament building of Westminster: 900 feet long, 340 feet high. Fontane commented:

> 'There is a disproportionateness between the height of the building and the height of the great southwest tower [of 'Big Ben']; endless ornaments which press forward everywhere, rob it of the character of beautiful simplicity and allow the whole, despite its huge dimensions, to appear mean and almost unworthy.'

Fontane was apparently already so anglicised that he adopted a pseudo-utilitarian perspective; as such he observed: 'One searches for a purpose to this ornateness and can find none other than that it is there, to swallow dust and smoke and to provide accommodation for many thousands of swallows' nests.'

So the proportion appeared as a disproportion in his eyes. Westminster as a design of power revolted Fontane, no matter how much he admired the English parliamentary system and its liberal spirit. What repulsed him finally was the attitude of the all-powerful, the self-promotion of the political. This is the first indication of the pattern of reasoning that he would maintain all his life, and which he would repeat even more pointedly with respect to the Germany of the Kaiser and its political boastfulness.

What remains impressive to this day about Fontane's London sketches and insights, his presentations of the milieu and his reflections, is their longevity. A classic example of this is his narrative, *Von der Weltstadt Straßen*, in which he put the atmosphere and background noise into words, translated street songs, and described what happens in one of the large London central post offices during an evening. And he stood there on Tower Hill, in the spring of 1858, listening to drummers and jokers, saw shy, starving child beggars and tarted up canaries offered for sale, and then this reflection: 'The Tower itself, the old site of rising and overthrown ambition, of power and crime, accompanies us, peering into this era like a stranger, like the ghost of itself, and only the recruiting sergeants, those with the colourful bands on their hats who just passed us by and keep watch for brave lads, who may have the desire to avenge Kanpur [Cawnpore] or dock at Peking, remind us that blood still remains the glue of world history.'

Whoever is given to such thoughts by London can leave it with confidence again.

8

Chelsea, for Example

Where to? Chelsea. Via detours, of course. At the moment, I am a long way from Chelsea, in New Oxford Street, which was lengthened as a form of firebreak in the mid-19th century through the slums that began here. I stand in front of one of the first shops to open in this eastward extension of Oxford Street, in 1857: James Smith & Sons Ltd, specialist shop for umbrellas and walking sticks of their own manufacture, founded in 1830.

The year is 1857. Baudelaire's *Fleurs du Mal* and Flaubert's *Madame Bovary* are published in Paris, and *Little Dorrit* by Dickens in London. And James Smith Jr establishes himself with in-house manufactured umbrellas and walking sticks in this building, aptly named 'Hazelwood House', on the corner of New Oxford Street and Bloomsbury Street. Dickens and Gladstone were to become clients, and African chieftains would have ceremonial maces made here because they were told they should rejoice in finally belonging to civilisation according to the rules of the British Empire. And being part of this civilisation required having a James Smith & Sons Ltd bespoke stick or umbrella, which could also be used as a parasol in central Africa. The business, according to the founder's great-great-grandson, has remained relatively unchanged.

Standing before this elegant assortment of hand-made umbrellas and sticks one feels downright shabby with one's own dime-a-dozen brollie. I do not know why the thought of Chelsea should suddenly come to me amidst this splendid display of umbrellas and walking sticks on the edge of Bloomsbury. I head toward the Embankment, again across Covent Garden, straight through its central area. Around nine o'clock in the morning. I notice once again how many Londoners make their way to the office with a cardboard cup of coffee in hand. It has a white lid to prevent spillage, with an opening from which they sip, never slowing their pace. A beauty approaches me; no, not dressed in yellow; she smiles, says something; I return the smile, start to respond with a few words when I notice she is speaking into an inconspicuous telephone mouthpiece dangling from her ear. After her I encounter almost no-one who is not speaking into such a wormlike extension. I pass small cafés, at which people are sitting at tables on which the unnaturally warm autumn sun falls, not speaking to each other, but rather clogging their mouthpieces with words.

To the Strand. Past the Savoy where Thomas Mann lodged in 1947 when he presented his lecture, 'Nietzsche's Philosophy in the Light of Recent History', in the Senate House of London University, or the 'former Ministry of Information', as he noted precisely. However, he was one of the few northern Germans who never found much that was positive in London.

Moving along, moving along. London is a city in which you pick things up in passing. Even if you spend one, two, or even three hours in both Tate galleries, in the National Gallery or the Royal Academy of Arts, you leave them and within three paces have forgotten you were ever there, amongst the Gainsboroughs and Turners, the Naum Gabos and the installation artists and Surrealists (as if there is any kind of art that is not surreal!), because 'outside', after a few steps, life is more colourful than all the paintings in these museums.

An Irish bagpiper, in a green, threadbare kilt, with a green scarf tied around his head, stands on the Embankment. He wears a sign asking for a small donation, as he cannot give full breath to his pipes due to toothache and has insufficient funds to visit a dentist.

So, off to Chelsea. District Line to Sloane Square. Whenever I am near Sloane Square, I stop by the Royal Court Theatre to see what is on. Even when it was closed for a long period and enveloped by scaffolding, I would stand in front of its empty display cases from time to time. I saw Alan Bennett's weakest piece, *Kafka's Dick* (1986), there in the mid-1980s. Yes, it really was about Kafka's – according to Bennett – modest genitalia. It was perhaps the worst piece, in terms of content, I have ever seen on a London stage, which says quite a bit. Roger Lloyd Pack played Kafka, and Geoffrey Palmer played a fictitious biographer of Kafka's named Sydney, an insurance agent (like the author) whose wife falls in love with Kafka on the stage. Roger Lloyd Pack acted as though stuck in a strait-jacket, and Mrs Sydney gave the impression she was in love with the strait-jacket of this accident insurance specialist, Kafka. Bennett's piece relocated Kafka on to a Pirandello-like stage.

There are years in London when you find yourself constantly going to the theatre; in others you frequent any number of museums; then again only concerts or opera or only concerts and opera by Handel, a year when you cannot help but visit the Handel memorial, a narrow house (Number 25) in Brook Street for the most corpulent composer in history, a joke of cramped conditions when compared to the house where he was born in Halle. George Friederic Handel: he is proudly called a Londoner, demonstratively adopted on every occasion. But the Westminster Council, which is responsible for Brook Street, did not see itself in a position to guarantee the future of this recently opened memorial, now privately financed. Jimi Hendrix lived in the neighbouring house; they have now been joined so you can move from Handel to Hendrix and back, from one world to another.

In my first London theatre year, I saw, at the Haymarket, a now legendary production of Peter Shaffer's *Amadeus* with Paul Scofield as Salieri and Simon Callow as Mozart and Felicity Kendal as Constanze. Peter Hall directed, and Harrison Birtwistle, no less, was responsible for the musical side. I avoided the film by Miloš Forman. I will never forget how the last four chords of Mozart's Masonic Funeral Music droned through the Haymarket Theatre at the end of the piece in painful volume and Birtwistle-esque distortion. Nor will I forget how Simon Callow played a Mozart who feels his own genius becoming horrifying.

Chelsea, then. Chelsea and South Kensington and Brompton, names of an obsession. Brompton Oratory, for example, where Oscar Wilde was supposed to be received into the Catholic Church in 1874. Everything was ready, except Wilde. He stayed away from the ceremony and instead sent the priest a huge bouquet of white lilies in apology. London has no streets more literary than Cheyne Walk and Cheyne Row in the heart of Chelsea. Leigh Hunt lived here, the great romantic essayist and friend of all writers, Dante Gabriel Rosetti, Algernon Swinburne, George Meredith, and in, Number 4, George Eliot with her young lover John Cross, whose attempted suicide during their Venice honeymoon was foiled by gondoliers on the Grand Canal. Most importantly, the misanthropic Carlyles lived here, Thomas and Jane. Their house has remained a jewel of Victorian charm. In order to write his multi-volume (and then still fragmented) biography of Frederick the Great without being disturbed, Carlyle had the loft converted to an atelier with a glass roof. Eerily enough, what Carlyle wrote in these heights Hitler had Goebbels read to him during the ruinous 'Götterdämmerung' of the last weeks of the Second World War in the bunker at the Reich Chancellery.

At the Carlyles', 5 Cheyne Row. Virginia Woolf tried to imagine what it must have been like in this house where Jane and Thomas got on each other's nerves throughout their marriage and yet could not live without each other. She was his first reader and he her hatefully beloved vexation. Domestic tyrant versus neurotic – both simultaneously suffering from their good fortune: that they had no children. Chopin was a guest here. And I ask myself, how long would the sounds and blue notes he might have plinked on the modest piano on a visit remain audible in this house. After all, they would have been appropriate to soothe the tensions in this floral papered room, if not to dissolve them entirely.

Carlyle reflected on greatness in this tall narrow house, about historic greatness, just like the great Swiss cultural historian Jacob Burckhardt did at the time in the narrow town of Basle. Carlyle had a sense of the heroic. Why else had he studied German, corresponded with Goethe and visited the battlefields on which Frederick the Great gambled with his kingdom?

Carlyle was seen as a dark, unapproachable figure during his walks, a figure who seemed to have come out of a novel by E T A Hoffmann, a loner who thought on a great scale and who despised what he deemed as average.

Chelsea – the name is supposed to be derived either from 'chalk wharf' or 'shelf of sand', once a fishing village two miles upstream of Westminster, still sought after in the 18th century for its healthy air, as Jonathan Swift noted in his *Journal to Stella* (1710–13). Chelsea was a place of tolerance, of freethinking. So it should come as no surprise that George Eliot would not only move here in the last phase of her life, but also set the most important passages of her last (and perhaps most significant) novel, *Daniel Deronda* (1876), here in Chelsea. Daniel, the adopted son of an English aristocrat, rescues Mirah Lapidoth during one of his lonely rowing outings on the tides of the Thames, which has a particularly malicious current at Chelsea. He brings her to a 'small house in Chelsea', where he is certain 'that he could appeal there to generous hearts, which had a romantic readiness to believe in innocent need and to help it.' Which in this case meant, to take in a young Jewish girl who had attempted suicide. Daniel Deronda recognises his destiny in Chelsea; here he determines to discover his own identity and to aid Mirah in her desperate search for her mother. In Chelsea, in the narrow house on the river, where popular legend claims the floods dance to the music of violins sunk in it, Mirah finds confidence in herself and her singing voice. Daniel takes a boat from Chelsea that carries him downstream on the Thames to the Jewish quarter of the East End, where he becomes aware of his own Jewish roots when he is strangely touched by the ritual sounds of prayer and song in a synagogue.

The year 1524 played a decisive role in the development of Chelsea. It was the year in which Sir Thomas More moved to Chelsea with his rather large family; he was England's most important humanist, the author of *Utopia* (1516) and numerous transcriptions of Lucretius, a friend of Erasmus, and also, initially of Henry VIII and his arch-schemer Cardinal Wolsey. More made Chelsea fashionable: his house claimed the geographic mid-point between the royal palaces at Greenwich and Hampton Court. Thomas More's life in Chelsea is reflected in a 1527 drawing by

Hans Holbein, showing Thomas More as Catholic patriarch in a high, noticeably bright room that nevertheless exudes cosiness, with his family around him, either before or after prayer. Books dominate the scene and a wall clock stands in the place where one would expect a crucifix. Holbein drew a scene of early middle class life, as the artist knew it from Augsburg and Basel. It is the room of a religious man of letters, who is openly and remarkably conscious of the times in which he lives; it is not offered to the beholder as the house of a great statesman. Chelsea as refuge, but also as a place for an intellectual and *paterfamilias* emancipated from the power of the state that he himself had begun to defend. Holbein's drawing is seen as a narrative, as a visual coded message about Chelsea.

Just how legitimate such a view of Holbein's precise sketch is, may be shown by a miniature watercolour by Rowland Lockey, painted between 1595 and 1600, which carries on the story told in Holbein's version. Lockey expands the right side of the picture and paints in Thomas More's descendants, as well as Henry Patenson, More's household fool who peers out from behind a curtain. Perhaps the most important Lockey addition is the view of the famous garden of More's estate, as well as the silhouette of London in the distance, which was praised by Wolsey and Henry VIII. Chelsea represented distance from the city, and yet touching distance, in Lockey's eyes. Chelsea meant gaining a natural perspective of the true scale of life's proportions: first comes the power of intimacy based on domesticity and secure faith; only then can one deal with matters of state, for which the coat of arms in the background of the picture serves as a reminder. Thomas More's grandson, boldly enough, commissioned this picture of Catholic harmony from Lockey. It was only thinkable in miniature; after all this was in the midst of the arch-Protestant Elizabethan era.

English illustrators seem to be gifted with the ability for storytelling. For example, Wilkie Collins opens his novel, *The Woman in White* (1859), which summons up a whole host of narrators, who are spread across three time periods, with the report of a drawing master who compares 'the small pulse of the life within me, and the great heartbeat of the city', London. In our own times, Peter Greenaway's first important film, *The Draughtsman's*

Contract (1982), depicts erotic entanglements on an English country estate around 1700 from the perspective and in the narrative of a shrewd master draughtsman.

But concerning Chelsea, and with George Bernard Shaw in mind, one is able to say: dialect is not spoken here, only pure intellect. In the meantime, however, this elevated form of spoken intonation has been broadly replaced by more or less ordinary 'plutocrat-speak'.

9

Hampstead as an Intellectual Way of Life

A place for actors, idlers, and hedonists with an elastic bank account; once also for intellectuals, who now can just about afford Camden Town, Kentish Town and Tufnell Park, but have moved out to Stoke Newington for the most part. And then there is Islington, which was once a gathering place for (financially) stranded Hampsteaders. Its intellectual climate profited a good decade ago from such Hampstead migrants, but has since become unaffordable for academics.

The myth of Hampstead: Evelyn Waugh called it a 'social indicator' if one was invited to parties in Hampstead. Once upon a time mineral springs were discovered here and Hampstead was declared a health spa. But the springs proved to be less than plentiful. What remained were smart houses next to massive relics of Victorian cravings for power and buildings more likely to remind one of New Orleans, of the south of France or of Italy. Here, for example, the Venetian ambassador built his residence in the 18th century. Daniel Defoe remarked around 1725 that Hampstead was in the process of becoming a city. In Hampstead, however, there are also houses that Virginia Woolf called boxes, cosy little constructions with light coloured plaster walls (from soft pink to sky blue, which is bearable only thanks to the predominance of magnolia), like those at the seaside, complete with appropriate bric-a-brac on the windowsills and mantelpieces.

It is hardly surprising that famous architects repeatedly chose to settle in an area with such architectural diversity. Walter Gropius was amongst them for a time, and Ernő Goldfinger. Not to mention artists: Piet Mondrian lived here. And when Henry Moore, Barbara Hepworth and Ben Nicholson opened their studios in Hampstead, this smart part of London became the centre of British sculpture.

But more than anything else, Hampstead became the mecca of the literati. From Wilkie Collins to Aldous Huxley, from D H Lawrence to Katherine Mansfield and from George Orwell to Edgar Wallace – they were with their own kind in this area and enjoyed the traces of country living still present in Hampstead, along with urban consciousness. In 1852 one of the most important Pre-Raphaelites, Ford Madox Brown, painted the scene. One sees tradesmen, builders, peddlers, strolling rich people and in the right-hand corner the two great scholars of the Victorian era, Thomas Carlyle and John Ruskin – harmony between labour and intellect, effort and elegance.

Hampstead: this is also 20 Maresfield Gardens where Sigmund Freud had to spend his last months in exile. This is where they sit, the furniture of all furniture, the real couch from Vienna's Berggasse, the desk overloaded with figurines. And it was here that his daughter, Anna, continued his work as a child psychologist and steered it in new directions. Her great book, *Wege und Irrwege der Kinderentwicklung* ('Normality and Pathology in Childhood') (1968) is a fruit of Hampstead, great prose on deep insights into the child's mind.

Freud wanted to die in freedom, in peace after 33 operations and persecution by the Nazi mob in Vienna. During his Channel crossing he dreamed that he, the king of the realm of the subconscious, would land in Pevensey like William the Conqueror in 1066. While Freud was in exile in Hampstead Stefan Zweig arranged for him to be visited by the young Salvador Dali, the most spectacular representative of the realm of the surreal. Freud appreciated his 'innocently fanatical eyes and undeniable technical mastery'.

Hampstead, first and foremost, is Hampstead Heath. What are Hyde Park and Kensington Gardens and all the green squares in comparison to the Heath, with Parliament Hill and the incomparable view of London, literally to Whitehall on a clear day, the Heath with Kenwood House where there are Rembrandts and one of the largest collections of paintings by Goethe's friend, Angelika Kauffmann? Literature has always developed on the Heath. The Romantics came here, 'to take note of people', as William Hazlitt, the great essayist of the early 19th century, said. This is where Doris Lessing and Alfred Brendel take their constitutionals; and at the edge of the Heath lives Michael Foot, once Leader of the Labour Party and author of numerous biographies, amongst them the most readable one on Byron.

Across from Hampstead Heath railway station is a small 24-hour grocery store run by Bengalis, which also contains a small post office and a newsagents. On an October day in the mid-1980s I was making my few purchases, and was about to reach for a packet of tea when I noticed on the other side of the shop a slender old man with snow-white hair, horn-rimmed spectacles and a coat that nearly reached the floor. He had just put his shopping basket down on the top of the freezer. He stood there in the middle of the shop and made notes in a small black book: Elias Canetti, without a doubt. He wrote and wrote, lost to himself and the world it seemed, and then left the shop still scribbling, the black notebook held close to his eyes, leaving the half-filled shopping basket behind where he had just been standing.

I went over to the freezer and the basket. And what did I see? On top of the packet of crispbread and some rice was a quite long shopping list, clearly Canetti's. 'Bananas', I read, and 'soap' and 'rice' twice underlined. Below that a sentence. 'Progress becomes *fatum* in the city' and: 'Trail comes from sensing'. I copied the sentences down in the margin of my newspaper, left the basket and list where they were, placed my own equally half-filled basked next to it and also left the shop empty-handed but enriched by the sentences of a Nobel Prize winner and crossed the road to return to the Heath.

Weeping willows fringe the western part of the Heath. Weeping willows with green tears. They extend to the Vale of the Heath, the valley of convalescence, the extension of the so-called Well Walk where one encounters the springs whose water was comparable to those taken by polite society in Bath or Tunbridge Wells. Around 1700, Well Walk became a proper promenade with music pavilions and dances in the so-called Great Room. But when increasingly 'rough' folk joined those promenading and Well Walk threatened to degenerate into the Gin Lane of North London, the Great Room was unceremoniously converted into a chapel.

It was in Well Walk that John Keats looked after his tubercular brother, Tom, in the last months of his life during the second half of 1818, and thereby contracted the disease himself. After Tom's death Keats remained in Hampstead, moving with a friend into one half of a whitewashed duplex on Wentworth Place, the other half of which the Brawnes would move into in the spring of the following year. Keats soon began to mention the elegant Fanny (same name as his sister!) in his letters, in which she seemed a bit aloof. That soon ended and the story of a love that would prove to be torturous took its course. They lived side by side, separated only by a wall; but this turned out to be impenetrable. They were allowed occasional walks on the Heath but only when chaperoned by one or two others. They saw the same trees in the garden, heard the same birds, Keats most probably the nightingale that inspired his famous ode, travelled the same path to the house and yet had to live separately. After all, who was Keats in the eyes of Fanny's family? A versifier, failed apothecary and medic, who preferred the company of obscure youths; a coughing dreamer of scant means whose poems had just been scathingly reviewed in a leading literary magazine (*Blackwood's Magazine*) – it was the autumn of 1818.

His heart 'in a blaze', is how Keats saw himself. He believed himself to be standing in a conflagration. When he could no longer bear the increasing emotional tension in Wentworth Place he took to his heels and fled to Shanklin on the Isle of Wight. From there he wrote to Fanny, to whom he had become secretly engaged before his departure, called her his 'Beauty', his hope, his everything. He had gone off London, he complained in his room with a sea view in Shanklin, and he did not dare return to Hampstead because being in the house in Wentworth Place would tear him apart.

When he did finally return, he took his time and went to Winchester initially, considered a side-trip to Teignmouth and eventually ended up in London's Fleet Street (Number 93) at the offices of the publishing house, Taylor & Hessey, from where he wrote to Fanny in Hampstead, uncertain whether he dared to return to 'this fire'. He dared, that poet marked by ill health. After all, the engagement could now be officially announced. His return brought about no change in his situation, which became more desperate from week to week.

He distracted himself by writing poetry and reading, but was 'occupied with nothing but you', his Fanny next door, whom he sent letter after letter, from door to door in a way. His health became more precarious. Again he fled, but this time, in mid-1820, only got as far as Kentish Town, near his friend the politically-aware Leigh Hunt, who was consumed with despair over the oppressively reactionary government of Lord Castelreagh. Amongst British men of letters, William Wordsworth, formerly an apologist for the French Revolution, sided with the reactionaries, to the horror of his young disciples.

The young Hampstead Romantics were far from being apolitical dreamers. They suffered during the political repression after 1815, yearned for far-reaching political reforms, which had failed to materialise by 1832 and thus came too late for most of them. Those who could afford it left England: Byron went first and wrote to his publisher, Murray, from Lake Geneva; 'Remember me to my friends in London. But I have none.' Shelley followed, as did Keats, deathly ill in September 1820, although Fanny Brawne had been allowed to care for him for a few weeks in Wentworth Place. Poet, love and death. Keats had lived just 26 years when he succumbed to his illness in the Piazza di Spagna in Rome in February 1821. On board the ship *Maria Crowther*, which was to bring him to Naples after a hellish sea voyage in the autumn of 1820, with Yarmouth and the Isle of Wight still in sight, Keats wrote to his friend, Charles Brown, that his sister Fanny and Fanny Brawne had become one and the same person in his mind's eye: 'The one seems to absorb the other to a degree incredible.'

He could no longer bring himself to write to his two Fannys, who had become one in his imagination, neither from Naples where he arrived half dead, nor from Rome. Instead he wrote to Fanny's mother, Mrs Samuel Brawne, and admitted to her that he dare not think of her daughter in his condition. And yet he had nothing more comforting with him than the pocket-knife in a silver case that she had given him as a farewell gift, in addition to her hair in a locket and a pocketbook bound in gold. He did not write to her, his beloved Fanny, because he feared she would answer. To see her handwriting and the Hampstead return address, according to Keats in his last letter to Charles Brown, would break his heart. And Fanny Brawne? She continued to live in Hampstead, lived with her memories, lived in Wentworth Place, unmarried, until she died 43 years after her fiancé's death.

Traveller, should you find yourself in Hampstead, inquire for the way to Wentworth Place in the shadow of weeping willows and think of a love so strong that other feelings might pale with envy. And should I now see, after leaving the Keats house once again after a recent visit, my Lady in Yellow, perhaps reading a volume of Keats' poems seated under a willow tree, I should have to go past her without a second thought.

At the age of 22, Keats had developed a theory of sorts in a few sentences in a letter, the meaning of which is debated by experts to this day. Keywords: negative capability. A year before his brother Tom's death, Keats wrote: 'Negative Capability, that is when man is capable of being in uncertainties, Mysteries, doubts, without any irritable reaching after fact & reason', for rational explanations, in other words. What did Keats mean by this?

Keats was not polemicising against the Enlightenment, never mind espousing a literary anti-enlightenment; he was a dedicated reader and admirer of Voltaire's. No, he understood negative capability to be part of enlightenment about human behaviour, as well as a specific posture: from time to time, on a case-by-case basis, man would have to allow doubts to remain doubts and mysteries to remain mysteries. He should not expect to be able to always explain everything; he would have to learn to exist in uncertainty and insecurity. As an example, Keats did not know why he was indifferent to Mozart's music ('I care not for white busts'), yet was kept awake at night by a tune of Mozart's.

'Capability' commonly refers to the *vita activa*, to the ability to do something, to the will to act. Keats' *capability*, in contrast, seems to have been pointed more to the *vita contemplativa*, to the sheer ability to persist in (mysterious) indecisiveness. *Negative capability* is a positive vote for the value of the unfathomable as the actual limit to intellectual experience.

And I have to admit that I never pass through Hampstead without thinking of Keats and of Fanny Brawne and of negative capability. There I forget about the Yuppies, and junkies, the smart set in London's Bohemia. Nor, in Hampstead, do I often think of Charles de Gaulle, who restlessly paced up and down here between 1940 and 1942, vexed that Churchill had made provision for his exile so far from the centre of power in Whitehall. I think of Keats, as he read Shakespeare and Milton, wracked with chills, hot flushes and coughing up blood, as he dreamed of the south and the mystery of love.

Perhaps poets really do have to love like that, tortured by love and fulfilled by such torture. After all, they do not love their fellow man (Keats admitted that he loved mankind, but not man), rather its phantom, and the 'belle dame sans merci' whom he was supposed to have encountered on the Heath when he was reading *King Lear*, which he greatly admired. Keats loved his sister in Fanny Brawne and in Fanny Brawne the woman as such, the inspiration that emanates from her, the unattainable. His *negative capability* was thus also a *negative attainability*. But one thing is attainable: the poem. It may be that it is created from words that are ultimately 'writ on water' as is inscribed on Keats' tombstone in Rome. In Hampstead, at least, you can believe they were written in green ink, ink derived from the tears of the weeping willows along the Heath.

En Route to a London Man of Letters

A t times it seems to me as though I had an appointment with authors I am currently reading. As it is now – with the most London-esque writer of the present day, with Peter Ackroyd. Because I am reading *London: The Biography* and am amazed about the definite article in the title. I want to speak with Ackroyd about this dumbfounding 'the'.

Our first encounter was years ago and took place in Birmingham. Ackroyd appeared to feel somewhat out of place in Birmingham, remaining in the vicinity of the main railway station, New Street, in order to be able to leave at any time. Birmingham did not please Ackroyd, nor the signing session (his Thomas More biography had just been published), nor the speech by the bookseller, nor the subsequent meal, the tasteless vegetables (he did not even touch the monkfish), the stale red wine, not to mention the weak coffee. He was not interested in the fact that Birmingham was in the process of blossoming, allowing the inner city to finally become a city centre (with funding from the European Development Fund). Birmingham had made its main square, Victoria Square, and several other areas 'fit for human beings' again in the last few years, explained the bookseller over dinner to his stocky, diminutive guest who was obviously not listening; presumably he was already in the middle of thinking about his next book.

At the time I noticed Ackroyd's hands, hands that rarely gestured, that could have been those of a sculptor; it is how I imagine Henry Moore's hands, articulate hands, pointing, creating, feeling their way. Ackroyd's hair appeared prematurely thinning, yet the remaining strands seemed unruly, subdued with the help of pomade and roughly combed back. And the eyes. Ackroyd's eyes did not peer, they penetrated; there was something raptor-like about them, very blue, almost youthful, where he himself appeared much older than he actually was. There was something tormented about this gaze. This was the man I wanted to encounter again. Because of the too definite article in the title of his London book.

In the newspaper I found a notice in the 'events' section that Ackroyd would read from *London: The Biography* in a large bookstore in Piccadilly. Today. The paper had even done him the favour of setting *The* in italic type. I set off by way of the diversions of various bus routes, which acquainted me with streets I had never seen before.

Ackroyd is something of a globetrotter between Islington and Kensington, Tower Hill and Walthamstow; because going from Islington to Kensington is like travelling once around the world and back again. One question poses itself particularly urgently in the case of Ackroyd: how much of London can a man take? Because after completing the 800-page effort of *London: The Biography*, Ackroyd, as his publisher's catalogue mentions, suffered a severe heart attack. This vigorous author naturally responded with ideas for further episodes of his London epic. He wants to write about the London of Daniel Defoe, that of William Turner and Shakespeare; but also about a subject that appears quite unrelated to London: he wants to attempt a biography of the Virgin Mary. But when you stop to consider there are 72 churches dedicated to Our Lady in London, then you cannot preclude the possibility that Ackroyd may interweave the Virgin's biography with that of London. For him, there is little that cannot be related to London.

Nothing that Ackroyd has written since his novel *Hawksmoor* (1985) would be conceivable without the background of London. *Hawksmoor* represents the sinister, bizarre London. Ackroyd takes on the subject of this stubborn architect, Nicholas Hawksmoor, portrayed in the book as a schizophrenic, whose most wilful work could probably be deemed to be the church of St George in Bloomsbury Way, completed in 1731 after a 15-year construction period. Horace Walpole called it a 'master-stroke of absurdity'. The bell tower consists of a pyramid, which Hawksmoor modelled on Pliny the Elder's description of the Mausoleum of Halicarnassus. King George I, clad in a Roman toga, stands atop the pyramid as St George. Ackroyd's Hawksmoor stands in front of his structure one night and wants to climb up to his George, in order to scream at London.

Ackroyd's monumental effort on London can be seen as a reflection of the mad ambition of Hawksmoor's projects. This ambition also covers in principle his biographies of T S Eliot (1984), William Blake (1995) and Thomas More (1998); primarily, everything he has written about Charles Dickens: a play and a television film, a coffee-table book and a voluminous biography (1990).

Dickens was the Homer of London, and Ackroyd seems to be of the opinion that his perspective of London is sufficient for several centuries. That was demonstrated by Ackroyd's fictional character, Spenser Spender, who as a television producer in Ackroyd's first work of fiction (*The Great Fire of London*, 1982), knows only one goal: to make a film of Dickens' great novel, *Little Dorrit*, set against the backdrop of modern-day London. Ackroyd's obsession with Dickens goes so far that in his 1999 novel, *The Plato Papers*, he has a fictitious orator named Plato tell Londoners episodes of their history and introduces Darwin's *On the Origin of Species* (1859) as a novel by Dickens!

How should one read *London: The Biography*? I would recommend, the same way that Alice handles mirrors in her Wonderland: you enter the book to see what is hidden within it. A project, in other words, that should be called: how does one get a city, *this* city, to speak? A metropolis whose infrastructure is now threatening to collapse for all its frenzied activity.

Among contemporary London authors, perhaps only Ackroyd would have dared to engage in this venture and write *the* biography of London personified. He is the urban Man of Letters, who repeatedly disappears in the rambling fabric of the city only to reappear in unexpected places. He speaks of the smells, the eating habits, the beggars and sex murderers of this city, of *The Beggar's Opera* and Newgate prison, of areas of town that he describes like the limbs of a body. Because this city-body has a quasi-erotic aura. Ackroyd once flirted with the country, bought a cottage in Devon; but if you believe what he writes, was utterly bored there. And was afraid. Of wild animals and of being assaulted by gangs of youths. That reminds me of the prototypical English professional eccentric of yore, Edith Sitwell, who was asked in a television interview in the early 1960s how she liked being on her country estate. Life was unbearable there. Why does she not then move back into town? Because she needed some-thing she could wholeheartedly despise – country life. No, you should not expect an English pastoral from Ackroyd. The only descriptions of nature in this biography are those of the flower markets of time immemorial and of a tree on a street corner. He has little time for the parks of this city. Nevertheless they belong to the body called London.

Ackroyd mentions a further project on occasion, and will most likely do so again at the conclusion of his reading today. Together with two architect friends of his he wants to find the buried Fleet River (Fleet Street is named for this 'mysterious' river) under Farringdon Road in the City. Ackroyd is a passionate advocate of the subterranean rivers of London. It is easy to understand why. They symbolise the narrative flow, which sus-tains the text of the best-selling *London*. And this river cannot be permit-ted to run dry.

He sits there, just like he did in Birmingham two years before his heart attack, except with a more tense expression I think, the reddish blond moustache carefully trimmed. He reads from the chapter entitled 'He shuld neuer trobell the parish no more': ' "Strate" in London was "strete" in Westminster. There was no standard or uniform pronunciation, in other words; it would have differed even from parish to parish.'

In the subsequent throng around Peter Ackroyd, in which he occa-sionally disappeared, I did not succeed in asking the question about the definite article in the title of his London opus. He eventually left the bookshop through the emergency exit accompanied by a woman easily two heads taller, dressed in eye-catching yellow.

10

Suburbia as Literary Locale – Notes from London's Suburbs

Where am I? Would I be writing these lines if I knew? Because one is most likely to live in that which one reads and writes. If I am somewhere in London, reading Martin Amis' novel *London Fields* (1989), then the revolting London of Martin Amis is undeniably closer to me than the London in which I am when I open the book, somewhere in a café in Bayswater or in Plaistow.

In *London Fields*, the narrator describes the movements of Keith Talent, criminal and offspring of a criminal, through Greater London, his forays in twilight, clear across endless suburbs. And what does one find there: a taster of the actual city and its aftertaste, bedroom communities with idyllic front gardens, meagre regeneration zones in the fight to survive in the City.

For me, London started many years ago in the suburbia of the east, where Greater London becomes Essex, in Northwood Avenue, Elm Park, in one of those endless terraces of small houses with loads of bric-a-brac on the mantelpieces and limited perspectives. At least there were flocks of seagulls who came to Elm Park in the autumn and winter in hope of bread crusts; at least there were seagulls until they were startled and chased away by dogs whose owners brought stale bread in carrier bags and scattered it around the few benches in the park.

The small house in which I lived smelled permanently of boiled whiting. Fish for the cats. My widowed landlady's cat was on a war footing with me and constantly hissed at me. Occasionally I hissed back. From my room I looked out on the bare weeping willows and elms of Elm Park, on the perfectly tended patch of garden, which contrasted remarkably with the gardens to the left and right, which were noticeable for their neglect or because they housed rusting car parts.

The recently widowed landlady of German origin, attractive despite her portliness and advanced years, yet petite bourgeois, was surrounded by a few admirers, elderly widowers in the road, who came by regularly 'just to check up on matters'. The arrival of a 24-year-old German in the little house of the blonde widow caused excitement, not just amongst the older widowers in Northwood Avenue. The neighbouring ladies began to gossip as well.

The counter clerk at the post office of Elm Park, who had noticeably more daring make-up from week to week and big hair reminiscent of the 1960s, cracked one day and asked me while I was purchasing stamps for the Continent whether I would come for a drink in the local pub that evening, but without my landlady. It was also this bold, tarted-up post-mistress who one day returned a letter to me that I had given her to weigh with the suggestion that I must have made an error in the address. It was a letter to Vienna, Palais Palffy, at the time the editorial department of the journal, *Literatur und Kritik*. I had written the word 'Austria' under 'Wien'. She thought I must have meant 'Australia'. It turned out that neither Wien nor Austria meant anything to her.

My first impression of Elm Park was confirmed in just a few weeks: here too, in these apparently harmless suburbs and not only in London proper, literature lay in the streets. The neglected garden to the right belonged to a little house with dirty curtains and junk in the front garden. Two children: rather shy; a woman, usually with dark circles under her eyes. The man was a lorry driver. Their marriage, perpetual arguments. The paper-thin walls allowed unintended aural witness. There was screaming, swearing, and cursing at each other. The children tended to be addressed only in commanding tones. Fridays around midnight: the moans of lovemaking. The morning after usually brought the sounds of breaking dishes.

So where does suburbia begin? In or after Crouch End or Stoke New-ington? Not in Richmond, but in New Malden. A real Londoner is able to sense these subtleties. They cannot be pinned down, cannot really be defined. No one would think to call Hampstead or Richmond, Brixton or even Kingston a suburb, but they would in the case of Croydon and Sidcup, as well as proverbial Surbiton. Hampton considers itself posh and Harrow on the Hill, Pinner and Stanmore are amongst the finest of the finest in the northern west.

If you consider the dreary architecture of many London suburbs, you are overcome with either melancholy or you agree with Francis Bacon's essay '*Of Building*' (1623) in which he writes that one should judge houses only on their utility. The building of aesthetically pleasing structures should be left to the poets: they can build them more cheaply – with words. Twice a week I pass the house in which Bacon was born in 1561, in Villiers Street, Embankment, as son of the Lord Keeper of the Great Seal: Bacon the philosopher who was so consciously economical with words in his essays, who was later, though perhaps not for that reason, elevated to Lord Verulam and then Viscount St Alban; who suddenly fell from grace when he was suspected of corruption; who died, deeply in debt, in the building of his thoughts.

There are former suburbs of London, which have long been absorbed into the core of the metropolis although they have retained some of their suburban character. Deptford is one of these areas. In the dockyards of Deptford Peter the Great (incognito), Pepys and John Evelyn once raised a pint together. This is where Christopher Marlowe was murdered, perhaps the most talented Elizabethan playwright after Shakespeare. More recently, this is where the Laban Centre for Movement and Modern Dance has been built in the middle of a totally derelict area by the two Swiss architects who were also responsible for the Tate Modern (Jacques Herzog and Harry Gugger). Extremely colourful outside, inside a func-tionalism that attempts to surpass itself.

No chance that I might accidentally run into my Lady in Yellow here. Not a shadow of a hope for yellow. More likely in Richmond or Kingston, where I could imagine she might be sitting reading on the concrete structure surrounding the Coronation Stone of Anglo-Saxon kings that can be found hidden there – reading a book with yellowing pages acquired in an antiquarian bookshop. No, at the Laban Centre you are more likely to see young women in white or raspberry-coloured track suits, their hair pulled back tightly, carrying gym bags and the ever-present blue plastic bottle of still mineral water.

Suburbia is where life is truly lived (in contrast to the office existence of the city); here one is at home, in that arid ordinariness, behind windows with aluminium frames, illuminated toadstools in the front garden, televisions on from morning till night. In suburbia the following are cumulatively found: banality, malicious gossip, rumours of all types, and violence.

No one captured this world more precisely and wittily that Hanif Kureishi in his novel *The Buddha of Suburbia* (1990). It is a world of sharply delineated ethnic districts, the tensions between them, a world of braggarts and idleness: 'In the suburbs people rarely dreamed of striking out for happiness. It was all familiarity and endurance: security and safety were the reward of dullness. I clenched my fists under the table. I didn't want to think about it. It would be years before I could get away to the city, London, where life was bottomless in its temptations.'

It is strange, however, when you live on the edge of suburbia south of the Thames in Surrey, amongst faux Tudor half-timbered architecture in the southwest district of London called Richmond. You feel like a Londoner, just barely, and already Surreyian with the promise of the country, that English landscape that Gainsborough so dearly loved to use as a background in his portraits, whilst it became the actual motif of John Constable and William Turner.

Richmond began to perk up during Henry VII's reign, when he named this area, originally Sheene, after his estates in Yorkshire, Rychemonde, and had a country seat built here. People moved here to escape the plague epidemics of urban London. Richmond was considered eminently fashionable in the 18th century. Those who held themselves in high esteem lived on the Green with its Theatre Royal (today the Richmond Theatre), which even then could offer many of the plays as a type of preview whilst still in rehearsal that would later be produced on the great stages of London's West End. James Boswell called this theatre the West End in Miniature. When the theatre opened, David Garrick, one of the most renowned actors of his time, wrote a special prologue for the occasion.

Richmond and its Green. This is where a proper palace once stood, where Elizabeth I died in 1603. And where, or at least in what was left of this palace, the Old Palace, Prince Metternich found refuge when he fled from Vienna in 1848. Disraeli visited him here, but the view out on to the Green impressed the later British Prime Minister more than the conversation with the man who had been the most powerful politician of Europe.

The border between Richmond and Kingston is a question of hyphens: Richmond-upon-Thames may use them, while convention dictates that Kingston upon Thames must make do without them. But what are hyphens compared with the parks that connect these two districts? Richmond Park above all, with its two and a half mile diameter and stock of over 350 tame fallow deer and 250 equally tame red deer. Their ancestors were hunted here by Charles I and Charles II, and the tame yet always somehow arrogant game still appear to be smug about it. Richmond Park is a miracle of landscape, with its lakes and heathland, the gentle hills and sudden drop-off toward Kingston Vale.

Virginia Woolf lived for some time with Leonard in Hogarth House in Richmond and founded their legendary publishing company, Hogarth Press, there. But in her letters, essays and diaries she says next to nothing about Richmond Park. It is notable that her second manuscript published by Hogarth Press pertained not to Richmond Park, but rather its counterpart, the cultivated Kew Gardens on the other side of Richmond.

For a time (particularly between 1915 and 1924), Richmond became a mecca for contemporary literature due to the Hogarth Press. Russian literature was represented, primarily Gorki and Chekhov; American literature made appearances, especially Robinson Jeffers and Gertrude Stein; but the Hogarth Press also featured Italo Svevo and Rilke's poems,

in addition to Sigmund Freud and John Maynard Keynes. English literature was represented by, among others, Robert Graves, Christopher Isherwood, Herbert Read, Edith Sitwell, Vita Sackville-West, H G Wells and,
of course, Virginia Woolf herself.

Botanical garden versus open nature: what Virginia Woolf achieved
with her short story *Kew Gardens* (1919) is comparable to what she herself
called 'moments of being': observations that transform into reflections
which in turn can then gain a little life of their own, lasting perhaps for a
few lines. Characters blossom *because* they remember, because they allow
themselves memories – of the first kiss, when the first red water lily was
painted in Kew Gardens. Simon, for example, remembers Lily, although
Eleanor walks next to him with her children. He is presumably reminded
of Lily precisely because *only* Eleanor and their mutual children are wan-
dering past the flower beds in Kew; is reminded of Lily's 'square silver
buckle at the toe' and of the dragonfly that 'went round and round'. If it
had settled 'on that leaf, the broad one with the red flower in the middle
of it, if the dragonfly settled on the leaf she would say "Yes" at once', and
he would have married her.

We are what we remember is the message in this short story, whether it
be, as it often was with early Virginia Woolf, a snail that reminds us of the
laboriousness yet steadiness of our progress. The snail is her counterfoil
to the permanent acceleration of life in the city, a symbol of deceleration;
and Kew Gardens at the edge of suburbia seem to her to be the ideal place
for such a slowing down.

Depending on the time of day, suburbs resemble a prologue and epilogue to the big city: in the morning they are the prologue to what awaits
commuters in the city; in the evening, the epilogue to what they survived
for better or worse during their day in the city. Only on weekends does
suburbia completely triumph over the city, leaving it behind for the tourists. Suburbia can probably be defined most meaningfully as that which
encompasses those parts of a city tourists will never enter. Suburbia lays
its inhabitants low with a strong dose of lethargy, lets them potter in
their gardens, in their fenced-off, heavily mortgaged illusions of space

and nature. The bric-a-brac is dusted and perhaps the photograph of the Queen as well. The estate car that reached the 36th instalment of repayment is loaded up with the weekend's shopping at the supermarkets on the edge of the suburbs that are as long as they are wide. You live your life in suburbia and come to terms with its insignificance.

Epilogue, or

The Path to Freedom with Variations on a Theme in Oscar Wilde's Poem 'Symphony in Yellow'

So that is how you read your way through a metropolis: from Picca-dilly to suburbia and back, from the Burlington Arcade along Saville Row, all the way to the economically deprived areas, which start with the beggars at the side entrance to Green Park Tube Station just down from the Ritz, and back. Always returning to what is referred to as the heart of the metropolis and what each Londoner or London visitor associates with a different place or locale. Perhaps with Somerset House on the Strand or the crystal heart by a Nigerian artist exhibited in the Museum of Mankind. Every once in a while, as I wander through London, I am overcome by the strong desire to stop passers-by at random and ask them for their life story and to write them down, or to go into a few of the innumerable offices and ask what they attempt to do here, what is happening at their desks, what fates are being decided in these computers.

An omnibus across the bridge / Crawls like a yellow butterfly.
London seems like a huge, artificially animated vaudeville theatre, like a colossal electronic machine full of remotely operated surveillance systems. London: that is attraction without flair, greatness without substance, a necropolis fresh as a daisy (you now have to cough up £2 if you want to

visit Marx's grave in Highgate). London, that is the name of a stubborn, unfinishable serial novel.

And, here and there, a passer-by / Shows like a little restless midge.
'I began a comedy, and burnt it because the scene ran into *reality*; – a novel, for the same reason. In rhyme, I can keep more away from facts; but the thought always runs through, through ... yes, yes, through.' Such was a diary entry by the young Byron on 17 November 1813. I am reading him again in Trafalgar Square, in the National Portrait Gallery, in an exhibition on the legend of Byron.

Because the scene ran into reality.
His maiden speech to the House of Lords sounded differently. When he was preparing for it, he wrote from No 8 St James's Street to Lord Holland: '... we must not allow mankind to be sacrificed to improvements in mechanism. The maintenance and well-being of the industrious poor is an object of greater consequence to the community than the enrichment of a few monopolists by any improvement in the implements of trade, which deprives the workman of his bread, and renders the labourer "unworthy of his hire".' After Byron absorbed such an excess of reality and had taken a stand on issues of weavers and Luddites in middle and northern England for the purposes of a scandalous performance, he could only be helped in digesting societal problems by verses about ravishing beauties and heroes addicted to conquest.

Big barges full of yellow hay / Are moored against the shadowy wharf
Who should be surprised that I would accidentally peer over her yellow shoulder, my Lady in Yellow, in front of a Byron portrait of all places? She is listening to it being described by a virtual exhibition guide *qua* audio guide; at least that is what I thought. Her hair seemed more luxuriant, wilder, more wiry in front of this portrait. Her yellow still more yellow. This yellow left me more bewildered than ever. What help was it to me that I had an invitation to Zarina Bhimji's film, *Out of the Blue*, in my

pocket? Virginia Woolf was little help either; she had never written about yellow, though she had about green and even blue. About the blue of water and campanulas and the pale blue of certain Madonna veils. And the dripping green – somewhere beyond nature. But this yellow, interspersed with tones of ochre, even Van Gogh could only have dreamed of it. In places a yellow that changes into a type of brocade gold, which Thomas Phillips wove with his paintbrush into Byron's Albanian costume.

Eye contact. A shadow of vague recognition flashes across her face. Elgar, she says and points to the earphones, which her leonine mane of hair repeatedly caused to slip. Elgar's Cello concert. With Jacqueline du Prè. This music is like paths to freedom, she said, despite the fact that she was obviously captured by this music, as she was by her yellow hues.

And, like a yellow silken scarf, / The thick fog hangs along the quay.
An hour later we were sitting in a Chinese restaurant. Mineral water, sparkling, roast duck with rice, bits of egg and orange sauce, matching several of my Lady in Yellow's hues. What was, will be, she said over her lemon sorbet and pulled a slim volume with a yellow-grey cover by Virginia Woolf from her National Gallery carrier bag: *The London Scene*!

Where upon I said, we should found it again, the Memoir Club, which the Woolfs joined in March 1920. For the meetings of the club, members wrote memoirs that they then read to each other.

She, more yellow than ever at this moment: Perhaps.

> I: 'Where do you come from? Where?'
> She: 'Where are you going?'
> I: 'From London to London'
> She: 'And back'

She insisted on separate bills, which plunged the Chinese waiter, like all British waiters, into embarrassment. We said our farewells, within sight of the dome of the English National Opera and St Martin-in-the-Fields. She took her multi-hued yellow and her voluminous hair into this aborted evening. And I went on my way, passing amongst others a fashion shop with the name 'Hope and Glory' and a sign in the window, 'special sale due to shop closure'. Someone pressed a notice for a concert in my hand: tomorrow in St John's Smith Square, Elgar's cello concert. The notice was yellow.

The yellow leaves begin to fade / And flutter from the Temple elms, / And at my feet the pale green Thames / Lies like a rod of rippled jade Paling prospects. And translation problems. In the end it all comes down to a translation problem: How does the red of the buses translate into the yellow of a butterfly? How the giant growth named London into a describable relationship? And the word 'lies' in Wilde's verse? Or even 'rod'? 'Lies' could mean untruths or resting here. 'Rod' could equally mean sceptre or an instrument of punishment. Instrument of punishment is not grabbed out of thin air. Wilde mentions the elms of the Temple, the innermost district of London's justice system. Wilde's style of love threatens to become a legal case at any time and eventually does so. Finally, did this supposedly innocent pale green of the Thames not lie and betray in his eyes?

I know that Oscar Wilde threw the chrysanthemum from his buttonhole through the yellow fog into the Thames at the time, in the hope that it would someday become a water lily; or the most yellow water lily of London; I know it since the bits of egg in the rice and the orange sauce at the Chinese restaurant.

Biographical Index

Adler, H G (1910–88): German-speaking poet, novelist and private scholar, born in Prague from where he emigrated to London in 1947 having survived Theresienstadt and Auschwitz. Author of major studies on the sociology of the concentration camps.

Bachmann, Ingeborg (1926–73): Austrian poet and author. The prestigious Ingeborg Bachmann Prize, awarded yearly in Klagenfurt, is named after her. It is one of the most important awards for German literature.

Beuys, Joseph (1921–86): German conceptual artist who produced work in a number of forms including sculpture, performance art, video art and installations. He is widely regarded as one of the most influential European artists of the second half of the 20th century.

Bhimji, Zarina (1963–): Ugandan artist. One of her latest works, *Out of Blue*, was commissioned and produced by Documenta 11, held in Cologne, Germany in 2002. For this work, Bhimji returned to Uganda to film the architecture, airports, and graveyards as well as the military barracks, police cells, and prisons of Amin's reign of terror. In her work she explores the politics and poetics of power and history through images rich in colour, texture and content.

Brendel, Alfred (1931–): Austrian pianist. He is widely regarded as one of the great classical pianists of the second half of the 20th century.

Brod, Max (1884–1968): German-speaking author, composer and journalist. A prolific writer in his own right, he is most famous as a friend, biographer and literary executor of Franz Kafka.

Canetti, Elias (1905–94): British-Austrian novelist, born in Bulgaria, who wrote in German and won the Nobel Prize for Literature in 1981 'for writings marked by a broad outlook, a wealth of ideas and artistic power'.

Cazals, Frédéric-Auguste (1865–1941): French master of 19th century posters and lithographs.

Derain, André (1880–1954): French painter and illustrator. Together with his friend, Henri Matisse, he was considered one of the leaders of the Fauvism movement. In 30 paintings in 1906 (29 of which are still extant), Derain put forth a portrait of London that was radically different from anything done by previous painters of the city.

Fontane, Theodor (1819–98): German novelist and poet. After years of writing on Britain, travel, history and political subjects, at the late age of 57 Fontane finally took to what he would be remembered for, the novel. His fine historical romance *Vor dem Sturm* (1878) was followed by a series of novels of modern life, notably *L'Adultera* (1882), a book about adultery which was considered so risqué that it took Fontane two years to find a publisher. In his novels, *Frau Jenny Treibel, Irrungen, Wirrungen* (1892) and *Effi Briest* (1894), he found his very own tone, yielding insights into the lives of the nobility as well as the 'common man'; his achievement there was later described as poetic realism. In *Der Stechlin* (1899), his last finished novel, Fontane adapted the realistic methods and social criticism of contemporary French fiction to the conditions of Prussian life.

Forman, Miloš (1932–): Czech-born American film director, actor and scriptwriter. His best known works include the screen adaptation (1975) of Ken Kesey's novel *One Flew Over the Cuckoo's Nest* (1962) which won five Academy Awards including one for direction, and *Amadeus* (1984) which won eight Academy Awards.

Freiligrath, Ferdinand (1810–76): German lyricist, poet and translator. For a short period he was a co-editor of the *Neue Rheinischen Zeitung* which was edited and published by Karl Marx and Friedrich Engels between 1848 and 1849). His translations included works by Robert Burns, and Victor Hugo. In 1847, Franz Liszt set Freiligrath's poem *O lieb, so lang du lieben kannst* to music. The song was later arranged by Liszt for solo piano as his *Liebestraume No. 3*, which subsequently became one of his most famous piano pieces.

Gabo, Naum (1890–1977): Russian-born American sculptor in the Constructivism movement and a pioneer of Kinetic Art. Gabo's main lasting influence has been in Britain where he lived in the 1930s and introduced Constructivism to a generation of artists including Barbara Hepworth and Ben Nicholson. Gabo's engineering training was key to the development of his sculptural work that often used machined elements. London's South Bank Centre is the location of the largest collection of Gabo's sculpture.

Goldfinger, Ernö (1902–87): Hungarian-born architect and designer of furniture, and a key member of the architectural Modern Movement after he had moved to the United Kingdom. His name was also the inspiration for the name of James Bond's opponent in the 1959 book *Goldfinger* (and the 1964 film of the same name) by Ian Fleming, his neighbour in London.

Grabe, John Ernest (1666–1711): Prussian-born Anglican divine. He came to England, settled in Oxford, was ordained in 1700, and became chaplain of Christ Church. His works, which show him to have been learned and laborious but somewhat deficient in critical acumen, include a *Spicilegium SS. Patrum et haereticorum* (1698-1699).

Grass, Günter Wilhelm (1927–): German author. Born in Danzig (now Gdan´sk, Poland), he has lived in Germany since 1945. In his fiction he frequently returns to the Danzig of his childhood. He is still best known for his first novel, *The Tin Drum* (1959) a key text in European magic realism. His works frequently have a strong political dimension, and Grass himself has been an active supporter of the Social Democratic Party of Germany. He won the Nobel Prize for Literature in 1999.

Gropius, Walter (1883–1969): German-born American architect and founder of Bauhaus, whose overriding principle was that 'form follows function'. In 1923, Gropius designed one of his most famous works, door handles, now considered an icon of 20th century design and often listed as one of the most influential designs to emerge from the Bauhaus.

Gugger, Harry (1956–): Swiss architect. A partner in the prestigious architectural firm of Herzog and de Meuron in Basel, he has designed such bold projects as the competition for the 2008 Olympic Stadium in Beijing. Worldwide attention has been drawn to the Tate Modern in London, a project directed by him and born from the transformation of a former power station.

Harry, Graf Kessler (1868–1937): German art collector, museum director, essayist, publicist, politician, diplomat and pacifist. He was dismissed as Curator of the Weimar Museum for exhibiting Rodin's erotic drawings. He is amongst the most fascinating figures in German cultural life during the transition time from empire to dictatorship.

Hebbel, Friedrich (1813–63): German poet and dramatist. His first tragedy, *Judith* (1841), made his name known throughout Germany. He won the Schiller Prize for his last work, the magnificently conceived trilogy *Die Nibelungen* (1862), consisting of a prologue, *Der gehornte Siegfried*, and the tragedies, *Siegfrieds Tod and Kriemhilds Rache*.

Heine, Heinrich (1797–1856): German poet. Heine is best known for his lyric poetry, much of which (especially from his earlier works) was set to music by lieder composers, most notably by Robert Schumann. Other composers who have set Heine include Franz Schubert, Felix Mendelssohn, Brahms, and Richard Wagner.

Henze, Hans Werner (1926–): German composer well known for his left-wing political beliefs. He left Germany for Italy in 1953 because of intolerance towards his politics and homosexuality. An avowed Marxist, Henze has produced compositions honoring Ho Chi Minh and Che Guevara.

Herzen, Alexander (1812–70): Pro-Western Russian writer and thinker known as the 'father of Russian socialism'. He is held responsible for creating a political climate leading to the emancipation of the serfs in 1861. His autobiography *My Past and Thoughts* (1924) is often considered the best example of that genre in Russian literature.

Herzog, Jacques (1950–): Swiss architect and co-founder of the Swiss architecture firm Herzog & de Meuron. The firm has designed such buildings as the Tate Modern, Allianz Arena Munich and are now completing the National Stadium in Beijing.

Hildesheimer, Wolfgang (1916–91): German author who incorporated the theatre of the absurd. He originally trained as an artist, before turning to writing.

Hoffmann, E T A (1776–1822): German author of fantasy and horror, a jurist, composer, music critic, draftsman and caricaturist. Hoffmann's stories were tremendously influential in the 19th century. His most famil-iar story is *Nussknacker und Mausekönig* (*Nutcracker and Mouse King*) (1816), which inspired Tchaikovsky's ballet *The Nutcracker* (1892). His story *Der Sandmann* (*The Sandman*) (1816) similarly inspired Delibes' ballet *Coppélia* (1870).

Hölderlin, Johann Christian Friedrich (1770–1843): German lyric poet. His work bridges the Classical and Romantic schools.

Jünger, Ernst (1895–1998): German author of novels and accounts of his war experiences. Throughout his whole life he had experimented with drugs such as ether, cocaine and hashish; and later in life he used mes-caline and LSD. These experiments were recorded comprehensively in *Annäherungen* (1970).

Kauffmann, Angelika (1741–1807): Swiss painter. A long-time friend of Sir Joshua Reynolds, she was one of the petitioners for and early members of the Royal Academy. In 1773 she was appointed by the Academy with others to decorate St Paul's Cathedral; and it was she who, with Biagio Rebecca, painted the Academy's old lecture room at Somerset House.

Kinkel, Gottfried (1815–82): German poet. His poetry is of the sweetly sentimental type which was in vogue in Germany in the mid-19th century. His best works were the verse romances, *Otto der Schütz, eine rheinische Geschichte in zwölf Abenteuern* (1846) which in 1896 went into its 75th edition, and *Der Grobschmied von Antwerpen* (1868).

Kinkel, Johanna (1810–58): German composer, writer, and revolution-ary. Her second marriage was to Gottfried Kinkel, whom she assisted in his literary work. Her autobiographical novel *Hans Ibeles in London* was not published until 1860, after her death.

Kleist, Bernd Heinrich Wilhelm von (1777–1811): German poet, dramatist and novelist. The Kleist Prize, a prestigious prize for German literature, is named after him.

Klopstock, Friedrich Gottlieb (1724–1803) was a German poet. While still at school, he had already drafted the plan of *Der Messias*, upon which his fame mainly rests.

Koeppen, Wolfgang (1906–96): German author, considered to be one of the most important of the post-war era. His best known works includes the trilogy of novels: *Tauben im Gras* (1951, *Pigeons on the Grass*), *Das Treibhaus* (1953, *The Hothouse*), and *Tod in Rom* (1954, *Death in Rome*).

Kramer, Theodor (1897–1958): Austrian lyricist. His lyrical, yet unromantic texts created strength and poetry from the sensitively-captured milieu of an outsider: the proletarians, vagabonds, tradesmen, labourers and prostitutes. His legacy comprises more than 10,000 poems.

Kraus, Karl (1874–1936): Austrian writer and journalist, known as a satirist, essayist, aphorist, playwright and poet. He is generally considered one of the foremost German-language satirists of the 20th century.

Lichtenberg, Georg Christoph (1742–99): German scientist, satirist and anglophile, most famous for his posthumously-published notebooks.

Meysenbug, Malwida von (1816–1903): German women's rights advocate and radical social critic. A friend of the philosopher Friedrich Nietzsche and the composer Richard Wagner, she was also a political confidante of many persecuted 19th-century authors and proponents of democracy.

Monti, Raffaelle (1818–81): Italian sculptor. He produced sculptures working in marble, but he also created in metals, porcelain, concrete and remained active in the applied arts. He was commissioned by the Merchants of London, for the 1851 Crystal Palace Exhibition, and sculpted the huge *Old Father Thames* of concrete using Portland cement. It now reclines at St. John's Lock, Lechlade.

Moritz, Karl Phillip (1756–93): German writer and intellectual. He was one of the founders of German classicism and psychological fiction. His travelogues and his essays on art and mythology were a particular influence on Goethe and his contemporaries.

Rilke, Rainer Maria (1875–1926): Generally considered the German language's greatest poet of the 20th century. His haunting images tend to focus on the problems of Christianity in an age of disbelief, solitude, and profound anxiety, themes that sometimes place him in the school of modernist poets. He wrote in both verse and a highly lyrical prose.

Rosenberg, Isaac (1890–1918): English poet of the First World War who was considered to be one of the greatest of all British war poets. His poems from the trenches are recognised as some of the most outstanding written during the First World War.

Schiller, Johan Caspar (1723–96): father of the German poet, philosopher, historian and dramatist Friedrich Schiller. A military surgeon, he was later in charge of the orchards of the Duke of Württemberg. Author of studies on applied economics, agriculture and arboriculture.

Schönberg, Arnold Franz Walter (1874–1951): Austrian-American composer. Many of Schönberg's works are associated with the expressionist movements in early 20th-century German poetry and art, and he was among the first composers to embrace atonal motivic development. Schönberg is particularly well-known as the innovator of the twelve-tone technique, a compositional technique involving tone rows.

Semper, Gottfried (1803–79): German architect, art critic, and professor of architecture, who designed and built the Semper Oper in Dresden

(1838–41). Beside the Dresden Opera House and a project for an opera house in Munich, later cannibalised by Wagner for the Bayreuth Festspielhaus, he designed works on any scale, from a baton for Richard Wagner to urban interventions like the re-design of the Ringstrasse in Vienna.

Simmel, Georg (1858–1918): One of the first generation of German sociologists. His studies pioneered the concept of social structure. Simmel writing in 1903 was critical of modern urban life, finding it incompatible with a positive urban culture.

Steiner, Franz Baermann (1909–52): Czech-born poet and anthropologist. He was a writer who, as an anthropologist, belonged to the English-speaking world, but as a poet, formed part of the German literary tradition. One of his longest and finest poems, *Gebet im Garten*, is a meditation on the death of his parents in extermination camps in 1942. Two collections of his poems appeared posthumously: *Unruhe ohne Uhr* (1954) and *Eroberungen* (1964), as did some of his anthropological writings in English. Much of his work remains unpublished.

Svevo, Italo (pseudonym of Aron Ettore Schmitz) (1861–1928): Italian businessman and author of novels, plays and short stories. He wrote the classic novel *La Coscienza di Zeno* (*Confessions of Zeno*) and published it himself in 1923. His tutor, James Joyce, championed its translation into French and publication in France.

Werfel, Franz (1890–1945): Austrian-Czech novelist, playwright, and poet who wrote in German. His true claim to international fame came in 1933, when he published *The Forty Days of Musa Dagh*, a chilling novel which first drew world attention to the Armenian genocide at the hands of the Turks.

Zangwill, Israel (1864–1926): English-born Zionist and writer. He wrote a very influential novel *Children of the Ghetto* (1892), and his play *The*

Melting Pot was a hit in the USA in 1908–09. Zangwill founded an organization called the Jewish Territorialist Organization in 1905, the aim of which was to create a Jewish homeland wherever possible. He died in 1926 after trying to create the Jewish state in such diverse places as Canada, Australia, Mesopotamia, Uganda and Cyrenaica.

Zweig, Arnold (1887–1968): German writer and an active pacifist. Zweig's pacifist novel *The Case of Sergeant Grischa* (1927) made him an international literary figure. The Soviet Union gave him the Lenin Peace Prize for his anti-war novels.

Zweig, Stefan (1881–1942): Austrian writer who wrote novels and short stories, and several biographies, of which the most famous is probably that of Mary Stuart in 1935. Zweig also wrote the libretto for several of Richard Strauss' operas.

Bibliography

Peter Ackroyd, *London. The Biography* (London: 2000).

——, *Dickens* (London: 1990).

——, *The Great Fire of London* (London: 1982).

H G Adler, *Die unsichtbare Wand* (Novel) (Vienna: 1989).

——, *Der verwaltete Mensch. Studien zur Deportation der Juden aus Deutschland* (Tübingen: 1974).

——, *Theresienstadt 1941-45. Das Antlitz einer Zwangsgemeinschaft. Geschichte, Soziologie, Psychologie* (Tübingen: 1955).

Martin Amis, *London Fields* (London: 1989).

Rosemary Ashton, *Exile & Asylum in Victorian England* (Oxford: 1986).

John Betjeman, *City of London Churches* Pitkin Guides (Andover: 1956).

Karl H Bohrer, *Die Idylle in der Wildernis. Szenen von Covent Garden*, in *Frankfurter Allgemeine Zeitung*, 20 September 1980.

John W Brennan, 'East End Stories. 13 Szenen aus dem Londoner Tagebuch', in *Schweizer Monatshefte* 80 (2001), pp 41–3.

Thomas Carlyle, *Reminiscences* (C E Norton: London: 1932).

Ian Cunningham, *A Reader's Guide to Writers London* (London: 2001).

Thomas De Quincey, *Autobiography* (David Masson, London: 1889).

Friedrich Engels, *Condition of the Working Class in England*, ed by David McLellan (Oxford, New York: 1993).

T S Eliot, *The Waste Land*, in *The Complete Poems and Plays* (London: 1969).

Theodor Fontane, *Ein Sommer in London* (Frankfurt am Main/ Leipzig: 1995).

Rüdiger Görner, *Streifzüge durch die englische Literatur* (Frankfurt am Main/ Leipzig: 1997)

Heinrich Heine, *Pictures of Travel*, tr by Charles Godfrey Leland (8th rev ed, Philadelphia: 1879).

Kirsten Hertel, *London zwischen Naturalismus und Moderne. Literarische Perspektiven einer Metropole* (Heidelberg: 1997).

Michael Hollington, 'Dickens the Flâneur', in *The Dickensian*, 77 (1981), pp 71–87.

Richard H Horne, *Memoirs of a London Doll* (London: 1846).

Ted Hughes, *Birthday Letters* (London: 1998).

Henry James, *The Complete Notebooks of Henry James* (New York/ Oxford: 1987).

Samuel Johnson, *A Dictionary of the English Language* (London: 1765).

Ernst Jünger, *Annäherungen. Drogen und Rausch. Sämtliche Werke* (Stuttgart: 1978). Vol II, p 127.

John Keats, *Letters. A Selection* (Robert Gittings. Oxford: 1970).

Charles Knight, *London*, Vols I–VIII (London: 1873ff).

Theodor Kramer, *Die Wahrheit ist, man hat mire nichts getan. Gedichte* (Herta Müller, Vienna: 1999).

Angela Krewani, '"Mind the Gap". Die Londoner U-Bahn in Film, Literatur, Malerei und Design', in *KulturPoetik* 2 (2002), pp 184–97.

Hanif Kureishi, *The Buddha of Suburbia* (London: 1990).

Cecil Day Lewis, *Poets' Corner. Westminster Abbey* (Manchester: NB).

Wolfgang Koeppen, *Nach Rußland und anderswohin. Gesammelte Werke* (Marcel Reich-Ranicki, Frankfurt am Main: 1986) Vol 4.

Kay Mann, *London: The German Connection* (Bridgewater/Somerset: 1993).

Ian McEwan, *Atonement* (London: 2001).

H V Morton, *The Heart of London* (15th Edition London: 1936).

Karl Phillip Moritz, *Werke*. Ed. by Horst Günther, Vol 2: Reisen (Frankfurt: 1993).

Adolf Muschg, 'Neither here nor There: The Alps. The Presence of Mountains in the London Tube' in *New Books in German* (Autumn 2002), p 20.

Gilda O'Neill, *My East End. Memories of Life in Cockney London* (London: 2000).

Samuel Pepys, *Tagebuch aus dem London des 17. Jahrhunderts*. Selected, translated and published by Helmut Winter (Stuttgart: 1980).

Christopher Ross, *Tunnel Visions. Journeys of an Underground Philosopher* (London: 2001).

W G Sebald, *Vertigo*, tr Michael Hulse (New York: 2000).

Percy B Shelley, *The Complete Poetical Works* (London: 1932).

Hilde Spiel, 'Morgenland der Orientalen. Eindrücke aus dem winterlichen London', in *Frankfurter Allgemeine Zeitung* (7 February 1981).

Italo Svevo, 'A Short Walk to Woolwich. Of Men and Things in Southeast London' in *Times Literary Supplement* (11 October 2002).

Paul Verlain, 'Aquarelle. (London-Gedichte)', in *Poetische Werke. Französisch und deutsch* (Sigmar Loffler, Frankfurt am Main / Leibzig: 1994), pp 221–31.

Malcolm Warner, *The Image of London. Views by Travellers and Emigres 1550–1920* (Barbican Art Gallery, London: 1987).

Georges Waser, 'London – City and East End', in *Neue Zurcher Zeitung* (2 September 1982).

Ben Weinreb with Christopher Hibbert, *The London Encyclopaedia* (London: 1983).

William Wordsworth, 'Composed Upon Westminster Bridge', in *The Complete Poetical Works* (London: 1959) Vol 18, p 178.

Oscar Wilde, *The Complete Works*, ed Vyvyan Holland (London: 1948).

Virginia Woolf, *The London Scene. Five Essays* (London: 1975).

Stefan Zweig, *Tagebücher*, ed Knut Beck (Frankfurt am Main:1984), pp 107–10.

ANTHONY TROLLOPE

SIR FRANCIS BACON

VIRGINIA WOOLF

HEINRICH HEINE

JOHN KEATS

THOMAS CARLYLE

T S ELIOT